The
Random House
Treasury
of
Humorous Verse

RANDOM HOUSE
New York

The
Random House
Treasury
of
Humorous Verse

EDITED BY

Louis Phillips

Originally published in 1995 as *The Random House Treasury of Light Verse*.

Library of Congress Cataloging-in-Publication Data
The Random House treasury of humorous verse / edited by Louis Phillips.
       p.   cm.
  Includes index.
  ISBN 0-375-70588-0
  1 Humorous poetry, American. 2. Humorous poetry,
      English.
I. Phillips, Louis.
PS595.H8R36   1995
811'.0808—dc20   95-18787
                           CIP

Manufactured in the United States of America

First Edition
March 1999
9 8 7 6 5 4 3 2 1

New York   Toronto   London   Sydney   Auckland

To the Sour Reader

If thou dislik'st the piece thou light'st on first,
Think that of all that I have writ the worst;
But if thou read'st my book unto the end,
And still dost this and that verse reprehend,
O perverse man! If all disgustful be,
The extreme scab take thee and thine, for me.

—Robert Herrick

for

William Rossa Cole

poet, anthologist, &, most of all, friend

Contents

Acknowledgments

Abook of this nature could not have been compiled without the advice and generosity of many persons. I would like to thank the following persons for their many kindnesses: William Cole, who shared with me his library and his knowledge; Bruce E. Newling, Bob McKenty, Willard Espy, Alma Denny, Ned Pastor, and Maureen Cannon, all members of the delightful Bards' Buffet; John Mella, editor of *Light*, the one publication in the United States devoted wholeheartedly to light verse; Robert Wallace, whose Bits Press has also kept light verse in America alive and well; Robert Milgrom, who hunted down a verse or two; Burnham Holmes, who graciously allowed me to use verses from his manuscript *The Song of the People: An Anthology of North American Indian and Eskimo Art & Poetry*; Armand Schwerner, who went out of his way to provide me with suggestions for Inuit and other verses to include; and X. J. Kennedy, one of the best light verse writers around. I am also grateful to Jesse Sheidlower, my editor at Random House, for his guidance, patience, and sense of humor.

Dear Reader

'Twas long ago, in Boston, Mass., I knew a wise old
    person.
(He was an advertising man named Edward K.
    McPherson.)
Esthetic problems he'd resolve in words I've not forgotten.
"It's all a question of taste," he'd say, "and your taste
                  is rotten."

How often I have found myself disputing with the thinkers
If works of art are good or bad or absolutely stinkers!
And very often I'd get out of arguments I'd got in;
"It's all a question of taste," I'd say, "and your taste
                  is rotten."

Many a man has read my rhymes and did not like a word
    of 'em;
And very many more there be who never even heard of
    'em.
I do not mind if you should find these poems misbegotten;
"It's all a question of taste," I'd say, "and your taste
                  is rotten."

—*Morris Bishop*

Introduction

Tell me not in joyous numbers
We can make our lives sublime
By—well, at least, not by
Dabbling much in rhyme.
—Stephen Crane

The desire to laugh, smile, grin, and chuckle—
at ourselves and others—is reflected in many
forms, in many media. One such form, often
neglected, is what is (sometimes disparagingly) re-
ferred to as "light verse." There are poets, critics, and
scholars in and out of academic settings—trained pro-
fessionals!—who claim to know everything there is to
know about light verse and who go about erecting
grand theories on the subject. Alas, I, for better or for
worse, am not one of those profound persons. I am
just out for a bit of fun. And I hope you are too.

I mean, just on the face of it, light verse should-
n't be too heavy, should it? It should be written with a
certain *je ne sais quoi,* and it should be read in high

1

spirits. Or, if we are not in a cheerful mood, it should lift our spirits or bring us a smile of wry recognition. A state of graceful delight is not to be scoffed at.

Of course, there are persons with deeper insights on the subject. In his introduction to *The Oxford Book of Light Verse* (first published in 1938), W. H. Auden declared: ". . . poetry which is at the same time light and adult can only be written in a society which is both integrated and free."

It sounds good, only I don't believe it's true. Light verse has been written by all sorts of people under all sorts of conditions—didn't the Romans compose magnificent epigrams under the most oppressive of emperors? The Deep South during the slave era was far from integrated and free, but consider the Negro Folk Rhymes that Professor Thomas W. Talley of Fisk University published in the early 1920s. A great many of those rhymes are certainly light—for example, "A Tom Cat":

> *My father had a big Tom cat*
> *That tried to play a fiddle.*
> *He struck it here, and he struck it there,*
> *And he struck it in the middle.*

I believe, however, that light verse writers are on the side of the values we call "civilized." The charac-

2

teristics attributed to civilization by Clive Bell apply to numerous realms of light verse: "From these primary qualities, Reasonableness and a Sense of Values, may spring a host of secondaries: a taste for truth and beauty, tolerance, intellectual honesty, fastidiousness, a sense of humor, good manners, curiosity, a dislike of vulgarity, brutality and over-emphasis, freedom from superstition and prudery, a fearless acceptance of the good things of life, a desire for complete self-expression and for a liberal education, a contempt for utilitarianism and philistinism, in two words—sweetness and light."

Drawing upon a deep sense of humor, tempered by a profound sense of injustice, numerous light verse writers inveigh against ineptitude and bureaucracy; some are frankly perplexed by sex and love; still others attempt to instruct us in an amusing and beguiling manner. Whoever wrote "The Multiplication Table in Rhyme for Young Arithmeticians" (circa 1865) was such a high-minded and didactic individual:

> *Eight times six are forty-eight,*
> *Their trees their doom with smiles await;*
>
> *Eight times seven are fifty-six,*
> *Their hues like dying dolphins mix.*

I would hope that no astute reader would confuse these two couplets with serious poetry—or even good light verse. But they have their use, I suppose, as does the following well-known example of mnemonics:

> Thirty days hath September,
> April, June and November;
> All the rest have thirty-one
> Except February alone,
> Which has four plus twenty-four
> And every leap year one day more

Other light verse makers, such as Samuel Hoffenstein (who, I believe, had a hand in scripting the film version of *Dr. Jekyll and Mr. Hyde* that starred Frederic March) are preoccupied with such playful games as the search for a rhyme for *orange*. One such attempt is his "Sad, Mad Song":

> Love flies out of the window
>   When I come through the door;
> When I come in through the window,
>   Reverse, and pour—
> So, partly serious, but more in jes',
> I try to find rhymes for oranges.*

*Nor is Samuel Hoffenstein the only light verse writer who has searched for that elusive rhyme for *orange*. I would like to direct the reader's attention to a verse by Arthur Guiterman

4

That's a pretty fair description of light verse: partly serious, but more in jest. But no subject is foreign to it. Not even death. How marvelous it is to look the Eternal Footman in the face and laugh. Many a lively verse maker has passed a pleasant rainy afternoon making up funny epitaphs. I am partial to one that appears on a tombstone in London Township, Michigan:

> *Here he lies,*
> > *My horse Bill.*
> *If he hadn't died,*
> > *He'd be living still.*

I submit that is an example of logic that is difficult to refute, though no doubt there are obstinate individuals who will try.

(p. 123). Also, the redoubtable Willard Espy, in his indispensable rhyming dictionary, *Words to Rhyme With* (Facts on File, 1986), includes his own contribution to the quest for "The Unrhymable Word: Orange":

> The four eng-
> > ineers
> Wore orange
> > brassieres
>
> And so the beat goes on.

5

One of the more powerful short poems of the twentieth century is Randall Jarrell's "The Death of the Ball Turret Gunner":

> From my mother's sleep I fell into the State,
> And I hunched in its belly till my wet fur froze.
> Six miles from earth, loosed from its dream of life,
> I woke to black flak and the nightmare fighters.
> When I died they washed me out of the turret with
> a hose.

There are many ideas that one might express about Jarrell's poem, but I doubt that many readers would suggest that the tone of the poem is light. It is a dark poem, bitter and matter of fact. Consider, by way of comparison, this anonymous poem about "The Dying Airman," which deals with roughly the same subject, but can hardly be called serious:

> A handsome young Airman lay dying,
>   And as on the aerodrome he lay,
> To the mechanics who round him came sighing,
>   These last dying words he did say:

> "Take the cylinders out of my kidneys,
>   The connecting-rod out of my brain,
> Take the cam-shaft from out of my backbone,
>   And assemble the engine again."

6

That is the light verse way. Or at least one of the ways.

To my way of thinking, defining light verse, like defining poetry itself—or humor itself, for that matter—is frequently an exercise in futility and is best left to persons who have more spare time and more government grants than I do. Most of us, however, know it when we see it or hear it. We sense the general lightness of it all. I know I said that I would make no grand pronouncements on the essential nature of light verse, but since I have grown fat eating my words, I'll take a wild stab: the differences between light verse and so-called serious poetry can be traced to their respective muses. Euterpe is the muse in charge of lyric poetry, whereas Thalia inspires comedy and bucolic poetry. We dare not woo two women in the same way, but they are both beautiful and worthy of our admiration.

The best approach, I feel, is to set all prejudice aside, open the present volume, and read with a generous spirit. Be prepared to laugh, to smile, to enjoy the great variety of forms and wide range of observations herein. Life is too short to always be taken seriously.

So make yourself at home and enjoy the good company here.

—*Louis Phillips*

ONE

The Children's Hour, or
some semblance thereof

The Walrus and the Carpenter

The sun was shining on the sea,
  Shining with all his might:
He did his very best to make
  The billows smooth and bright—
And this was odd, because it was
  The middle of the night.

The moon was shining sulkily,
  Because she thought the sun
Had got no business to be there
  After the day was done—
"It's very rude of him," she said,
  "To come and spoil the fun!"

The sea was wet as wet could be,
  The sands were dry as dry.
You could not see a cloud, because
  No cloud was in the sky:
No birds were flying overhead—
  There were no birds to fly.

The Walrus and the Carpenter
  Were walking close at hand:

They wept like anything to see
    Such quantities of sand.
"If this were only cleared away,"
    They said, "it *would* be grand!"

"If seven maids with seven mops
    Swept it for half a year,
Do you suppose," the Walrus said,
    "That they could get it clear?"
"I doubt it," said the Carpenter,
    And shed a bitter tear.

"O Oysters, come and walk with us!"
    The Walrus did beseech.
"A pleasant walk, a pleasant talk,
    Along the briny beach:
We cannot do with more than four,
    To give a hand to each."

The eldest Oyster looked at him,
    But never a word he said:
The eldest Oyster winked his eye,
    And shook his heavy head—
Meaning to say he did not choose
    To leave the oyster-bed.

But four young Oysters hurried up,
  All eager for the treat:
Their coats were brushed, their faces
    washed,
  Their shoes were clean and neat—
And this was odd, because, you know,
  They hadn't any feet.

"A loaf of bread," the Walrus said,
  "Is what we chiefly need:
Pepper and vinegar besides
  Are very good indeed—
Now, if you're ready, Oysters, dear,
  We can begin to feed."

"But not on us!" the Oysters cried,
  Turning a little blue.
"After such kindness, that would be
  A dismal thing to do!"
"The night is fine," the Walrus said,
  "Do you admire the view?"

"It was so kind of you to come!
  And you are very nice!"
The Carpenter said nothing but
  "Cut us another slice.

I wish you were not quite so deaf—
    I've had to ask you twice!"

"It seems a shame," the Walrus said,
    "To play them such a trick,
After we've brought them out so far,
    And made them trot so quick!"
The Carpenter said nothing but
    "The butter's spread too thick!"

"I weep for you," the Walrus said:
    "I deeply sympathize."
With sobs and tears he sorted out
    Those of the largest size,
Holding his pocket-handkerchief
    Before his streaming eyes.

"O Oysters," said the Carpenter,
    "You've had a pleasant run!
Shall we be trotting home again?"
    But answer came there none—
And this was scarcely odd, because
    They'd eaten every one.
                        —*Lewis Carroll*

There Was a King

There was a King and he had three daughters,
And they all lived in a basin of water;
    The basin bended,
    My story's ended.
If the basin had been stronger
My story would have been longer.
               —*Anonymous*

There Was an Old Woman Tossed in a Blanket

There was an old woman tossed in a basket,
    Seventeen times as high as the moon;
But where she was going no mortal could tell,
    For under her arm she carried a broom.
"Old woman, old woman, old woman," said I,
    "Whither, oh whither, oh whither so high?"
"To sweep the cobwebs from the sky,
    And I'll be with you by-and-by."
               —*Anonymous*

The Bells of London

Gay go up and gay go down
To ring the bells of London Town!

Bull's eyes and targets,
Say the bells of St. Marg'rets.

Brickbats and tiles,
Say the bells of St. Giles.

Halfpence and farthings,
Say the bells of St. Martin's.

Oranges and lemons,
Say the bells of St. Clement's.

Pokers and tongs,
Say the bells of St. John's.

Tin kettles and saucepans,
Say the bells of St. Anne's.

Old father Baldpate,
Say the slow bells of Aldgate.

You owe me ten shillings,
Say the bells of St. Helen's.

When will you pay me?
Say the bells of Old Bailey.

When I grow rich,
Say the bells of Shoreditch.

When will that be?
Say the bells of Stepney.

I'm sure I don't know,
Says the great bell at Bow.

—*Anonymous*

Counting Song

One, two,
Buckle my shoe;
Three, four,
Knock at the door;
Five, six,
Pick up sticks;

Seven, eight,
Lay them straight;
Nine, ten,
A big fat hen;
Eleven, twelve,
Dig and delve;
Thirteen, fourteen,
Maids a-courting;
Fifteen, sixteen,
Maids in the kitchen;
Seventeen, eighteen,
Maids in waiting;
Nineteen, twenty,
My plate's empty.

—*Anonymous*

Sing a Song of Sixpence

Sing a song of sixpence, a pocket full of rye;
   Four and twenty blackbirds baked in a pie.
When the pie was opened, the birds began to sing:
   Wasn't that a dainty dish to set before the king?
The king was in the countinghouse, counting out
     his money;

The queen was in the parlor, eating bread and
    honey;
The maid was in the garden, hanging out the
    clothes,
When down came a blackbird and snapped off
    her nose.

—*Anonymous*

Noah Built a Ark

Didn' ol' Noah build him a ark,
Build it outen hick'ry bark;
Animals come in one by one,
Cow a-chewin' a toas'ed bun.

CHORUS

Hallelu, Hallelu,
Hallelujah to de Lamb;
Hallelu, Hallelu,
Hallelujah to de Lamb;
Hallelu, Hallelu.

—*Anonymous*
(American Folk Rhyme)

Simple Simon

Simple Simon met a pieman
  Going to the fair;
Says Simple Simon to the pieman,
  "Let me taste your ware."

Says the pieman to Simple Simon,
  "Show me first your penny";
Says Simple Simon to the pieman,
  "Indeed I haven't any."

Simple Simon went a-fishing,
  For to catch a whale;
All the water he had got
  Was in his mother's pail.

Simple Simon went to look
  If plums grew on a thistle;
He pricked his finger very much,
  Which made poor Simon whistle.

        —*Anonymous*
        (Mother Goose Rhyme)

There Was a Crooked Man

There was a crooked man,
    And he walked a crooked mile,
He found a crooked sixpence
    Against a crooked stile;
He bought a crooked cat,
    Which caught a crooked mouse;
And they all lived together
    In a little crooked house.

—Anonymous

Rethinking a Children's Story

We have been so wrong in judging Simple Simon
it would take a nine-man court to rule in his favor.

He was really a mystic
searching for a Holy Land he called the Fair.

The Pieman thought only of money
and so it is no wonder he refused to give aid.

We should have sensed something was wrong
when Simon was convinced he'd catch a whale.

Go left, go right, take any road to anywhere,
is what Simon would tell us.

Sooner or later, you'll hear
carnival music, and see the ferris wheel turn.

Maybe it is turning, now, out on your lawn
between the raindrops and upon the air.

It does not take
science-fiction to explain the fourth dimension.

Rub your eyes, and be happy, and cheer
yourself with immaculate prayer.

Reason lives within reason.
It is the hand on the lever that stays on the
        ground.

Above it ride children and Simon
who spin like colored stones above the Fair.

We have never before
condemned a man who gives away his ware.

I wonder: to what ends will we go
when we pass out of light

and in the new dark ages
forget what science came among us to explore.

If our modern houses still had widow's walks,
the ladies of the universe would watch

sea and space, and rejoice
if it was Simon's hand that steered their loved
ones home.

                              —*Dick Allen*

Temptation, Temptation, Temptation

Temptation, temptation, temptation,
Dick Barton went down to the station,
Blondie was there, all naked and bare,
Temptation, temptation, temptation . . .

—*Anonymous*
(English Nursery Rhyme)

There Was a Little Girl

There was a little girl, she had a little curl
  Right in the middle of her forehead;
And when she was good, she was very, very good,
  And when she was bad, she was horrid.

—*Henry Wadsworth Longfellow*

from *A Song About Myself*

There was a naughty Boy,
    And a naughty Boy was he,
He ran away to Scotland
    The people for to see—
        Then he found
        That the ground
        Was as hard,
        That a yard
        Was as long,
        That a song
        Was as merry,
        That a cherry
        Was as red—
        That lead
        Was as weighty,
        That fourscore
        Was as eighty,
        That a door
        Was as wooden
        As in England—
So he stood in his shoes
    And he wonder'd,
    He wonder'd,

He stood in his shoes
And he wonder'd.
—*John Keats*

For a Cultured Child Weeping

Snivel
not,
civil
tot.
—*Richard Moore*

The Minister in the Pulpit

The minister in the pulpit,
He couldn't say his prayers,
He laughed and he giggled,
And he fell down the stairs.
The stairs gave a crack,
And he broke his humphrey back,

And all the congregation
Went "quack, quack, quack."
—*Anonymous*
(Scottish Nursery Rhyme)

Chicken Skin Trousers

I walked ten steps outside the gate,
   Which brought me to the ditches,
There I found some chicken skins
   To mend my leather britches.
If there had been no chicken skin,
I could not mend my trousers then.

—*Anonymous*
(Chinese Nursery Rhyme
translated by Isaac Taylor Headland)

Jump Rope Rhyme

Order in the court,
    The judge is eating beans.
His wife is in the bathtub
    Counting submarines.

—*Anonymous*

Counting Out Rhyme

Cinderella
Dressed in yella
Went downtown
    To buy some mustard.
On the way
    Her girdle busted.
How many people
    Were disgusted?
One-two-three-four-five-six-seven . . .

—*Anonymous*

Instant Stories

These books of stories come with blanks
in crucial spots, making wacky poets of us all.
My giggling daughters accost me, demanding
words they'll write out in the flimsy pads:

"Give me a noun . . . give me a color . . .
a country where you'd like to be."

They read back what I've written, draw me in
to my wild and random complicity:

> We hopped in the beat-up _tomato_
> and cruised down the _chartreuse_ highway,
> with dreams of wild nights in _Nepal._

Another day I hear my snickering girls
safely hunched in the cave of their room;
they finish still more of the riddled tales,
plugging in crude and forbidden terms:
snot and _bitch_ and _balls._
I want some way to tell them,
without their really hearing,
how there is no need for whispers,
how all that we mouth
comes roaring down to sameness:

Willy-nilly, shilly-shally,

> I left my _fried_ house and the yard was _dust_.
> The clouds _rattled_ on my _red stance_.
> Close around were the _distant_ piles of _doom_.
> —Stephen Corey

Twinkle, Twinkle, Little Bat!

> Twinkle, twinkle, little bat!
> How I wonder what you're at!
> Up above the world you fly,
> Like a tea-tray in the sky.
> —Lewis Carroll

Backyard Night, August

> Firefly, airplane, satellite, star,
> How I wonder which you are?
> —William Cole

Twinkle, Twinkle, Little Star

Twinkle, twinkle, little star,
How I wonder what you are?
Up above the world so high,
Like a diamond in the sky.

Well, I'll tell you, little star,
I can't tell you what you are;
With the smoke and haze and pall
I'm not sure you're there at all.
            —*Frank Jacobs*

Street Smart

At a year old my son saw, really saw,
for the first time, a streetlight. *Moon,*
he said, happy to see on his corner
the white globe from picture books—
brighter even than he'd imagined.
I was sorry he thought a pedestrian
object like that the moon.

I took it seriously. I'd failed
to provide him an understanding

of a major poetic symbol, capable,
as it was, of changing size and shape and color—
large red harvest moons, cold thin slices
of winter moons. The moon controlled the
     tides . . .

Moon, he said, pointing at that sad
city streetlight, and clapped his hands
like a wind-up toy. Now, years later,
when I travel, I look out my motel
window and see dry leaves blowing
in spirals across the highway
and headlights, little moons—

                              —*Ginny MacKenzie*

Three Brats

Where the dumptruck left its load
Of crushed stone to build a road,
Ag and Og, those reckless twins,
Rolled and romped with foolish grins,
Somersaulting in hot tar.
No one now knows where they are,
But, recalling as we drive

How they used to be alive,
In our throats we feel a lump
Every time we hit a bump.

Hacking with his home computer,
Clever Aloysius Booter
Cracked a six-star secret code,
Made the Pentagon explode,
Caused a ghastly guided missile
Down upon his house to whistle,
And reduced to ash and feces
Planet earth and all its species.
Al reluctantly stopped tappin'.
"Hell," he said, "it had to happen."

In the steaming hot tub Kurtz
Surreptitiously inserts
Pirhanas starved till good and mean
Just to help Aunt Jo come clean.
                    —*X. J. Kennedy*

Little Willie

Little Willie—
Pair of skates—
Hole in the ice—
Golden gates.

Willie saw some dynamite;
Couldn't understand it quite.
Curiosity never pays;
It rained Willie seven days.

Little Willie on the track
Heard the engine squeal.
Now the engine's coming back;
They're scraping Willie off the wheel.

Little Willie from the mirror
   Sucked the mercury all off,
Thinking, in his childish error,
   It would cure the whooping cough.
At the funeral his mother,
   Weeping, said to Mrs. Brown:
"'Twas a chilly day for Willie
   When the mercury went down!"

Willie fell down the elevator—
Wasn't found till six days later.
Then the neighbors sniffed, "Gee whizz!
What a spoiled child Willie is!"

—Anonymous

Making Toast at the Fireside

Making toast at the fireside,
Nurse fell in the grate and died,
But what makes it ten times worse,
All the toast was burnt with Nurse.

—Anonymous

Billy

Billy, in one of his nice new sashes,
Fell in the grate and was burnt to ashes.
Now, although the room grows chilly,
I haven't the heart to poke up Billy.

—Harry Graham

Aunt Eliza

In the drinking well
   Which the plumber built her,
Aunt Eliza fell.
   We must buy a filter.

          —*Harry Graham*

My Daughter as the Bull of Salamanca

(*für unsere Maikäferpump*)

Now one, she stands off to the side of the lawn,
   fuming:
the days of her life are still unnumbered. Fat-assed
June bugs sidle to the coliseum's archèd gate.
Cheers go up from the bystanders—tiger lilies
taking in the morning Vineyard sun.
Her breath puffs the dust of the corrida;
she snorts at the picadores, lifts a hoof
and reddens, balking at the dandelion wars.
She cocks an angry eye—the furrow of her brow
is set. When she lights on the crimson scarf,

35

she bows her head and plows along not looking—
still on all fours, aiming for gore
or nuzzlement, toward the unassuming
matador—just me, who's come to the backyard
to see if she wants lemonade to drink.

—*William Allen*

Old Dog Queenie

Old Dog Queenie
Was such a meanie,
She spent her life
Barking at the scenery.

—*Langston Hughes*

Piggy-back

My daddy rides me piggy-back.
My mama rides me, too.
But grandma says her poor old back
Has had enough to do.

—*Langston Hughes*

Revenge

Sy an' I went to de circus;
Sy git hit wid a rollin' pin.
Sy git even wid dat white man's circus—
Sy buy tickets but he didn' go in.

—*Anonymous*
(American Folk Rhyme)

Overindulgence

Some very small children
From Collingbourne Ducis
Imbibed by the gallon
The Concord grape's juices.

They took so much in
That it tinted their skin
To a hue that was close
To the color that puce is.

—*Bruce E. Newling*

Rhyme for a Child Viewing a Naked Venus in a Painting

He gazed and gazed and gazed and gazed,
Amazed, amazed, amazed, amazed.
—*Robert Browning*

Chickamy, Chickamy, Crany Crow

Chickamy, chickamy, crany crow,
I went to the well to wash my toe.
When I came back one
Of my black-eyed chickens was gone.
—*Anonymous*
(American Folk Rhyme)

The Woman
Who Lived Backwards

There was an old woman who lived in reverse:
She died in a crib and was born in a hearse.

In driving her car (in reverse gear of course),
She always made sure it was pushed by a horse.

Her garden grew tall with potatoes and peas,
So tall that their top leaves grew down to her
    knees.

She fizzled and sputtered when things were
    correct,
But whistled and hummed when her new car was
    wrecked.

The food she devoured (like ice cream and pork)
Refined her until she had legs like a stork.

She'd often set fistfuls of money on fire.
Guess what! The next day her bank balance was
    higher.

She read eighty books in the space of one
    summer,
And—wouldn't you know—in the fall she was
    dumber.

Her house was so spotless by noon every Friday
She brought in some trash just to make things
    more tidy.

She travelled each evening to where she'd been
    hired
And worked very hard so as not to be tired.

And then the next morning she'd hurry home
    fresher
To write a critique of her foe, M.C. Escher.

She turned on the light before going to bed,
Then slept with bare feet and a blanketed head.

She didn't get married but split in two pieces,
Then one of her went off to live with her nieces.

The other grew older till she was a baby.
And all of this story is partly true, maybe.

                                    —*John J. Brugaletta*

Little Bo-Peep

Little Bo-Peep
Has lost her sheep
   And thinks they may be roaming;
They haven't fled;
They've all dropped dead
   From nerve gas in Wyoming.

—Frank Jacobs

Uncle

Uncle, whose inventive brains
Kept evolving aeroplanes,
Fell from an enormous height
On my garden lawn last night.
Flying is a fatal sport;
Uncle wrecked the tennis court.

—Harry Graham

41

The Pessimist's Forecast

Monday's child is sad of face;
Tuesday's child will lose the race;
Wednesday's child has a row to hoe;
Thursday's child is full of woe;
Friday's child has futile strife;
Saturday's child has a mournful life;
While the child that's born on the Sabbath day
Will find that life is dull and gray.

—*Franklin P. Adams*

~ TWO ~

Man Is for Woman Made, or
love, lust, marriage, &
several variations thereof

Man, Man, Man

Man, man, man is for the woman made,
And the woman made for man;
As the spur is for the jade,
As the scabbard for the blade,
As for digging is the spade,
  As for liquor is the can,
So man, man, man, is for the woman made,
  And the woman made for man.

As the scepter's to be swayed,
As for Night's the serenade,
  As for pudding is the pan,
  As to cool us is the fan,
So man, man, man, is for the woman made,
  And the woman made for man.

Be she widow, wife or maid,
Be she wanton, be she staid,
Be she well- or ill-arrayed,
  Shrew, slut, or harridan,
Yet man, man, man, is for the woman made,
  And the woman made for man.

—*Anonymous*

Chinook Song

I don't care
If you desert me.
Many pretty boys are in the town.
Soon I shall take another one:
That is not hard for me!

> —*Anonymous*
> (Chinook Song
> translated by Franz Boas)

Upon Julia's Clothes

Whenas in silks my Julia goes,
Then, then, methinks, how sweetly flows
That liquefaction of her clothes.

Next, when I cast mine eyes, and see
That brave vibration, each way free,
O how that glittering taketh me!

> —*Robert Herrick*

Upon Julia's Speedos

Whenas in Speedos Julia goes,
Their fabric seemeth to expose
The wonders it doth juxtapose!

Next, when I cast mine eyes and see,
That Lycra stretching each way free,
Tumescence overtaketh me!
—*John Clarke*

Song

Pious Selinda goes to prayers,
  If I but ask a favour;
And yet the tender fool's in tears,
  When she believes I'll leave her.

Would I were free from this restraint,
  Or else had hope to win her!
Would she could make of me a saint,
  Or I of her a sinner!
—*William Congreve*

Fatal Love

Poor Hal caught his death standing under a spout,
Expecting till midnight when Nan would come out,
But fatal his patience, as cruel the dame,
And curs'd was the weather that quench'd the
    man's flame.

Whoe'er thou art, that read'st these moral lines,
Make love at home, and go to bed betimes.
           —*Matthew Prior*

Miss Buss and Miss Beale

    Miss Buss and Miss Beale
    Cupid's darts do not feel.
    How different from us
    Miss Beale and Miss Buss.
           —*Anonymous*
(Cheltenham Ladies College, Late Nineteenth Century)

Compensation

Weep not for little Léonie,
Abducted by a French *marquis*.
Though loss of honor was a wrench,
Just think how it improved her French!
—*Harry Graham*

It Was a Lover and His Lass

It was a lover and his lass,
　With a hey, and a ho, and a hey nonino,
That o'er the green corn field did pass.

CHORUS

In springtime, the only pretty ring time,
When birds do sing, hey ding a ding, ding:
Sweet lovers love the spring.

Between the acres of the rye,
　With a hey, and a ho, and a hey nonino,
These pretty country folks would lie.

This carol they began that hour,
    With a hey, and a ho, and a hey nonino,
How that a life was but a flower.

And therefore take the present time,
    With a hey, and a ho, and a hey nonino,
For love is crownèd with the prime.

—*William Shakespeare*

Spring

When daisies pied and violets blue
    And ladysmocks all silver-white
And cuckoobuds of yellow hue
    Do paint the meadows with delight,
The cuckoo then, on every tree,
Mocks married men; for thus sings he,

            Cuckoo;
Cuckoo, cuckoo: Oh word of fear,
Unpleasing to a married ear!

When shepherds pipe on oaten straws,
    And merry larks are plowmen's clocks,

When turtles tread, and rooks, and daws,
   And maidens bleach their summer smocks,
The cuckoo then, on every tree,
Mocks married men; for thus sings he,

             Cuckoo;
Cuckoo, cuckoo: Oh word of fear,
Unpleasing to a married ear!
             —*William Shakespeare*

New Words for an Old Saw

I love the girls who don't,
   I love the girls who do;
But best, the girls who say, "I don't . . .
   But maybe . . . just for you . . ."
             —*Willard Espy*

Samson and Delilah

As he pushed the pillars apart,
   Samson was appalled;
For just before the palace fell in,
   Delilah said "He's bald!"
      —*Spike Milligan*

Written in an Ovid

Ovid is the surest guide
  You can name, to show the way
To any woman, maid or bride,
  Who resolves to go astray.
      —*Matthew Prior*

Andrew Marvell

Higgledy-piggledy
Marvell the Lyricist
Said to coy mistress, "Our
Time we can't take."

To which the nameless lass
Cold-shoulderistical
Answered, "Oh, Andy, I've
Such a headache."
—*Anthony Harrington*

Naïf

"Make love, not war." One can, sweet simple boy?
I know the girl who tried it. Back at Troy.
—*John Frederick Nims*

Sigh No More, Ladies

Sigh no more, ladies, sigh no more,
    Men were deceivers ever,
One foot in sea and one on shore,
    To one thing constant never:

Then sigh not so, but let them go,
    And be you blithe and bonny.
Converting all your sounds of woe
    Into Hey nonny, nonny.

Sing no more ditties, sing no more,
   Of dumps so dull and heavy;
The fraud of men was ever so,
   Since summer first was leafy:

Then sigh not so, but let them go,
   And be you blithe and bonny,
Converting all your sounds of woe
   Into Hey nonny, nonny.
                    —*William Shakespeare*

Still to Be Neat

Still to be neat, still to be dressed,
As you were going to a feast;
Still to be powdered, still perfumed;
Lady, it is to be presumed,
Though Art's hid causes are not found,
All is not sweet, all is not sound.

Give me a look, give me a face
That makes simplicity a grace;
Robes loosely flowing, hair as free;
Such sweet neglect more taketh me

Then all th' adulteries of art.
They strike mine eyes, but not my heart.
          —*Ben Jonson*

A Woman's Song, About Men

First I lowered my head
and for a start I stared at the ground
for a second I couldn't say anything
but now that they're gone
I raise my head   I look straight ahead   I can
          answer:

They say I stole a man
the husband of one of my aunts
they say I took him for a husband of my own
          lies
          fairy tales
          slander
It was him, he
lay down next to me
But they're men
which is why they lie

That's the reason
and it's my hard luck.

—*Anonymous*
(Inuit Song
translated by Armand Schwerner)

A Medical Student Named Jones

A medical student named Jones
Learned all about all of the bones,
    The muscles, the senses,
    The nerves, and the menses,
And the nurses' erogenous zones.

—*Laurence Perrine*

Soldier, Won't You Marry Me?

Soldier, soldier, won't you marry me?
It's O a fife and drum.
How can I marry such a pretty girl as you
When I've got no hat to put on?

Off to the tailor she did go
As hard as she could run,

Brought him back the finest was there.
Now, soldier, put it on.

Soldier, soldier, won't you marry me?
It's O a fife and drum.
How can I marry such a pretty girl as you
When I've got no coat to put on?

Off to the tailor she did go
As hard as she could run,
Brought him back the finest was there.
Now soldier, put it on.

Soldier, soldier, won't you marry me?
It's O a fife and drum.
How can I marry such a pretty girl as you
When I've got no shoes to put on?

Off to the shoe shop she did go
As hard as she could run,
Brought him back the finest was there.
Now, soldier, put them on.

Soldier, soldier, won't you marry me?
It's O a fife and drum.

How can I marry such a pretty girl as you
And a wife and baby at home?
                —*Anonymous*

A Negro Love Song

Seen my lady home las' night,
    Jump back, honey, jump back.
Hel' huh han' an' sque'z it tight,
    Jump back, honey, jump back.
Hyeahd huh sigh a little sigh,
Seen a light gleam f'om huh eye,
An' a smile go flittin' by—
    Jump back, honey, jump back.

Hyeahd de win' blow thoo de pine,
    Jump back, honey, jump back.
Mockin'-bird was singin' fine,
    Jump back, honey, jump back.
An' my hea't was beatin' so,
When I reached my lady's do',
Dat I couldn't ba' to go—
    Jump back, honey, jump back.

Put my ahm aroun' huh wais',
    Jump back, honey, jump back.
Raised huh lips an' took a tase,
    Jump back, honey, jump back.
Love me, honey, love me true?
Love me well ez I love you?
An' she answe'd, " 'Cose I do"—
    Jump back, honey, jump back.
                    —*Paul Laurence Dunbar*

Marriage Couplet

I think of my wife, and I think of Lot,
And I think of the lucky break he got.
                    —*William Cole*

Fungible:
Interchangeable, Replaceable

One fury alone has God found inexpungeable;
The wrath of a woman who finds herself fungible.
                    —*Willard Espy*

Sally, Sally Waters, Sprinkle in the Pan

Sally, Sally Waters, sprinkle in the pan,
Hie Sally, hie Sally, for a young man,
    Choose for the best
    Choose for the worst
Choose for the prettiest that you like best.

       —*Anonymous*

Around the Corner

Around the corner,
    And under a tree,
The handsome major
    Made love to me.

He kissed me once—
    He kissed me twice—
It was a naughty thing to do
    But it was very nice!

       —*Anonymous*

Marilyn, When She Dresses Finely

There is none like thee among the dancers
—*Ezra Pound*

My Marilyn, oh when she dresses fine-
ly, dons her low-cut gown and thus displays
that bosom fair for which poor poets pine
and stammer helpless pleas, oh when she plays
the game of flaunt and flash, wears a skirt
upslashed to free the favor of her thigh,
and lets her leopard-patterned high heels flirt,
what blessings she bestows upon the eye!
But not yet done, my love begems her lobes
with spark and dazzle, slips on sequined gloves,
sprays on scents that stir with opiate strobes
the poet's hapless nose, and when she moves—
pity these poor plodding would-be prancers!
There is none like she among the dancers.

—*David Lunde*

The Ruined Maid

"O 'Melia, my dear, this does everything crown!
Who could have supposed I should meet you in
    Town?
And whence such fair garments, such prosperi-ty?"
"O didn't you know I'd been ruined?" said she.

"You left us in tatters, without shoes or socks,
Tired of digging potatoes, and spudding up docks;
And now you've gay bracelets and bright feathers
    three!"
"Yes: that's how we dress when we're ruined," said
    she.

"At home in the barton you said 'thee' and 'thou,'
And 'thik oon,' and 'theäs oon,' and 't'other'; but
    now
Your talking quite fits 'ee for high compa-ny!"
"Some polish is gained with one's ruin," said she.

"Your hands were like paws then, your face blue
    and bleak
But now I'm bewitched by your delicate cheek,
And your little gloves fit as on any la-dy!"
"We never do work when we're ruined," said she.

"You used to call home-life a hag-ridden dream,
And you'd sigh, and you'd sock; but at present you
    seem
To know not of megrims or melancho-ly!"
"True. One's pretty lively when ruined," said she.

"I wish I had feathers, a fine sweeping gown,
And a delicate face, and could strut about Town!"
"My dear—a raw country girl, such as you be,
Cannot quite expect that. You ain't ruined," said
    she.

—*Thomas Hardy*

Naughty But Nice

My arms around her taper waist
Her lovely form I pressed,
Her beauteous face reclining
Upon my manly chest.
I kissed her twice upon the lips,
I wish I'd done it thrice.
I whispered, Oh it's naughty,
She said, It is so nice.

—*Anonymous*
(Music Hall Song)

Jenny Kissed Me

Jenny kissed me when we met,
Jumping from the chair she sat in.
Time, you thief! who love to get
Sweets into your list, put that in.
Say I'm weary, say I'm sad;
Say that health and wealth have missed me;
Say I'm growing old, but add—
                                    Jenny kissed me.

—*Leigh Hunt*

Jenny Merely Kissed Me

Jenny kissed me when we met.
She, adorned in silk and satin,
Told me, "That is all you get;
And as you leave, don't let the cat in."
Retrospection makes me glad:
Dread disease perhaps thus missed me.
God knows what I might have had
Had Jenny more than merely kissed me.

—*Bruce E. Newling*

A Summing Up
of Lord Lyttelton's
"Advice to a Lady"

Be plain in dress, and sober in your diet;
In short, my deary, kiss me, and be quiet.
—*Lady Mary Wortley Montagu*

Miscalculation

In Lent, as a penance,
   A woman in Gissing
Denied herself dancing,
   Carousing, and kissing.

"Besides," she confessed,
   "I can do with a rest."
One assumes God is pleased,
   But her boyfriend is missing.
—*Bruce E. Newling*

Bobby Shaftoe

Bobby Shaftoe's gone to sea,
  Silver buckles on his knee.
    (chink, chink, chink, chink)
He'll come back and marry me,
  Bonny Bobby Shaftoe.

Bobby Shaftoe's bright and fair,
  Combing down his yellow hair.
He's my own for ever mair,
  Bonny Bobby Shaftoe.

Bobby Shaftoe's tall and slim,
Always dressed so neat and trim.
The lassies they all peek at him,
  Bonny Bobby Shaftoe.

Bobby Shaftoe's gettin' a bairn
For to dangle on his arm.
And to sit upon his knee,
  Bonny Bobby Shaftoe.

—Anonymous
(Scottish Folk Song)

Comin Thro' the Rye

I

Comin thro' the rye, poor body,
   Comin thro' the rye,
She draigl't a' her petticoatie,
   Comin' thro' the rye!

CHORUS

O, Jenny's a' weet, poor body,
Jenny's seldom dry:
She draigl't a' her petticoatie,
Comin thro' the rye!

II

Gin a body meet a body
   Comin thro' the rye,
Gin a body kiss a body,
   Need a body cry?

III

Gin a body meet a body
   Comin thro' the glen,
Gin a body kiss a body,
   Need the warld ken?

—*Robert Burns*

On Not Being Able to Read My Wife's Handwriting

I think of my wife's penmanship as a race
Of dwarves drowning in a cursive swamp, or
Lost, hands waving, as consonants rush face
To face into unmitigated vowels. On the door
To our refrigerator one early morning note, or
A map of Tasmania with spasmodic X's
Which might mean kisses or malfunctioning T's.
Oh, Momma, Momma, why didn't you warn me:
"Never marry a woman whose handwriting
You cannot read." Full-blown capital R's
Turned on their sides. My wife has either
Run off with the plumber (or is it carpenter?)
To inaugurate correspondences from Paris,
Or she wishes me to purchase for supper
Hornet butter, three pounds of javelins, and/or
One large rat to stab behind the arras.
Am I holding her message upside down? Possibly.
Now I shall suffer in suspense all day until night
To discover the full-mouthed truth of her scrawl.

—*Louis Phillips*

Reflections on
Reading the Tabloids

The Prince of Wales has lost Diana;
   their romantic bubble's burst.
He has the charm of an iguana—
   still, I wish he'd met me first.
                  —*Gail White*

I Dream of Jeannie
with the Light Blue Hair

My observation's keen; I know
         it's true
In nature, that there's seldom
         hair of blue;
And eyelids, I've observed, are
         rarely green
To start with; yet such oddities
         are seen
On many women; and their lips,
         once red,
Show lavender or pink; it's
         even said

That *some* will paint their fingernails
                with gold,
Or puce, or silver. Furthermore
                I'm told
That such things are attractive to
                the male:
Let's take a poll at Harvard
                or at Yale.
                —*William Cole*

Office Friendships

Eve is madly in love with Hugh
  And Hugh is keen on Jim.
Charles is in love with very few
  And few are in love with him.

Myra sits typing notes of love
  With romantic pianist's fingers.
Dick turns his eyes to the heavens above
  Where Fran's divine perfume lingers.

Nicky is rolling eyes and tits
  And flaunting her wiggly walk.

69

Everybody is thrilled to bits
    By Clive's suggestive talk.

Sex suppressed will go berserk,
    But it keeps us all alive.
It's a wonderful change from wives and work
    And it ends at half past five.

—Gavin Ewart

Dust to Dust

After such years of dissension and strife,
Some wonder that Peter should weep for his wife;
But his tears on her grave are nothing surprising—
He's laying her dust, for fear of its rising.

—Thomas Hood

To Cloe

I could resign that eye of blue
    Howe'er its splendor used to thrill me;
And even that cheek of roseate hue—
    To lose it, Cloe, scarce would kill me.

That snowy neck I ne'er should miss,
  However much I've raved about it;
And sweetly as your lip can kiss,
  I *think* I could exist without it.

In short, so well I've learned to fast
  That, sweet my love, I know not whether
I might not bring myself at last
  To—do without you altogether.
                    —*Thomas Moore*
        (translation of a poem by Martial)

News Item

Men seldom make passes
At girls who wear glasses.
        —*Dorothy Parker*

Dorothy Parker Update

Men often lose their senses
Over girls with contact lenses.
        —*Dorothy Dreher*

Further Updates on an Unending Bulletin

I heard a woman mutter:
Glasses or no glasses,
It neither hinders nor hurts,
For men will make passes
At anything in skirts.
                —*Anonymous*

Eyeglasses or No . . .

Men often get amorous
With gals who are mammarous.
                —*Bob McKenty*

Miss Emily Regrets

Said Emily Dickinson
to Thomas Higginson:

"I have met you twice
and that shall suffice."
—*Dorothy Dreher*

Overheard at a
Feminist Conference

Sisters, this may sound ominous,
But we all have a touch of the mom in us.
—*Richard Moore*

General Review of the
Sex Situation

Woman wants monogamy;
Man delights in novelty.
Love is woman's moon and sun;

Man has other forms of fun.
Woman lives but in her lord;
Count to ten, and man is bored.
With this the gist and sum of it,
What earthly good can come of it?

—Dorothy Parker

To Lucasta, Going to the Wars

Tell me not, Sweet, I am unkind
    That from the nunnery
Of thy chaste breast and quiet mind,
    To war and arms I fly.

True, a new mistress now I chase,
    The first foe in the field;
And with a stronger faith embrace
    A sword, a horse, a shield.

Yet this inconstancy is such
    As you too shall adore;
I could not love thee, Dear, so much,
    Loved I not Honor more.

—Richard Lovelace

Lucasta Replies to Lovelace

Tell me not, friend, you are unkind,
    If ink and books laid by,
You turn up in a uniform
    Looking all smart and spry.

I thought your ink one horrid smudge,
    Your books one pile of trash,
And with less fear of smear embrace
    A sword, a belt, a sash.

Yet this inconstancy forgive,
    Though gold lace I adore,
I could not love the lace so much
    Loved I not Lovelace more.

        —*G. K. Chesterton*

The Cudgeled Husband

As Thomas was cudgeled one day by his wife,
He took to his heels and fled for his life:
Tom's three dearest friends came by in the
    squabble,

And saved him at once from the shrew and the
      rabble;
Then ventured to give him some sober advice—
But Tom is a person of honor so nice,
Too wise to take counsel, too proud to take
      warning,
That he sent to all three a challenge next
      morning.
Three duels he fought, thrice ventured his life;
Went home, and was cudgeled again by his wife.

—Jonathan Swift

Cause and Effect

On his death-bed poor Lubin lies;
    His spouse is in despair;
With frequent sobs and mutual cries,
    They both express their cares.

"A different cause," says Parson Sly,
    "The same effect may give:
Poor Lubin fears that he may die;
    His wife, that he may live."

—Matthew Prior

Ex-wife

You wonder why
I'm grieving?

She said goodbye
Without leaving.
—*Edmund Conti*

Some Kiss Hot

Some kiss hot.
  Some kiss cold,
Some don't kiss
  Until they're told.

Some kiss fast,
  Some kiss slow,
Those that don't kiss,
  I don't know.
    —*Anonymous*

Conceivably, the Compleat History of Human Sex

Adam and Eve,
I believe,
Were the start of it.

Everyone since,
I'm convinced,
Played a part in it.
—*Kenneth Leonhardt*

Postcard to the Poet from a Jilted Bridegroom

She just ran off with some Miami bum.
Please cancel the epithalamium.
—*Gary Lutz*

20 Questions, or
Animal, Vegetable, or Mineral

SF

That patch of long-stemmed dandelions with
Their round white heads, one eye
Peering out of all that ticklish fuzz on each
One swaying in this summer breeze across
Connecticut this morning looks suspiciously
Like a patch of small delighted aliens
Just happened on our planet to take in the sun.

             —*Dick Allen*

from *Critters*

The Hode

The Hode is hairy.
Very.

That fact alone
is known.

The Loll

The Loll lies long and loose and lazy in the sun,
as if what he hankers for and what he has were
    one.

Stay back! For in another way perhaps he lies.
Your image glitters in all eighty of his eyes.

The Zing

The clan of the microscopic Zing
is puzzling.

One Zing unzips into two, the two into four;
and soon, all kin, there are thousands more.

But of course there can't
be father, mother, sister, brother, cousin, uncle, or
    aunt.

All Zings just are, familially speaking,
one and the same Zing.
                —Robert Wallace

Offer It Up

He prayeth best who loveth best
All creatures great and small.
The Streptococcus is the test—
I love him least of all.

—Anonymous

Doodle-bug

Doodle-bug!	Doodle-bug!	Come git sweet milk.
Doodle-bug!	Doodle-bug!	Come git butter.
Doodle-bug!	Doodle-bug!	Come git co'n bread.
Doodle-bug!	Doodle-bug!	Come on to Supper.

—Anonymous
(American Folk Rhyme)

The Life of a Gnat

The life of a gnat is so simple and straight,
as she crawls in the palm of your hand.
She's born in the dawn in the heart of the dew
and she dries out her wings in the sun.
Then she flies with her love,
tiny tiny love,
with her love, only hers,
tiny love, but true.

The moon rolls through the sky in the night
all alone in the wind and the dark.
She knows where she goes she has only got one,
and revolves in the light of her love.
Once a year in his arms
reeling round the sky
with her love, only hers
clasped in the arms of her sun.

The life of a girl is nothing like that,
though I wish and I dream that it were.
I look for the one that will set me afire
or dance me all day in the wind.
I would swim through the sky
if I thought he were there.

I would fly through the air
to capture my lonely desire.

I'd fly through the air like a gnat or a moon
to capture my lonely desire.
—*Andrew Glaze*

Fleas

Adam
Had 'em.
—*Anonymous*

The Flea

Mark but this flea, and mark in this,
How little that which thou deny'st me is;
Me it sucked first, and now sucks thee,
And in this flea, our two bloods mingled be;
Confess it, this cannot be said
A sin, or shame, or loss of maidenhead;
    Yet this enjoys before it woo,

And pamper'd swells with one blood made of
    two,
And this, alas, is more than we would do.

Oh stay, three lives in one flea spare,
Where we almost, nay more than married are.
This flea is you and I, and this
Our marriage bed, and marriage temple is;
Though parents grudge, and you, w'are met
And cloistered in these living walls of Jet.
    Though use make thee apt to kill me,
    Let not to this, self-murder added be,
    And sacrilege, three sins in killing three.

Cruel and sudden, hast thou since
Purpled thy nail, in blood of innocence?
In what could this flea guilty be,
Except in that drop which it suckt from thee?
Yet thou triumph'st and say'st that thou
Find'st not thyself, nor me the weaker now.
    'Tis true, then learn how false, fears be:
    Just so much honor, when thou yield'st to me,
    Will waste, as this flea's death took life from
        thee.

—John Donne

Great Fleas

Great fleas have little fleas upon their back to bite
     'em,
And little fleas have lesser fleas, and so *ad
     infinitum*.
The great fleas themselves in turn have greater
     fleas to go on,
While these again have greater still, and greater
     still, and so on.

—*Anonymous*

The Termite

Some primal termite knocked on wood
And tasted it, and found it good,
And that is why your Cousin May
Fell through the parlor floor today.

—*Ogden Nash*

The Book-Worms

Through and through th' inspirèd leaves,
   Ye maggots, make your windings;
But O, respect his lordship's taste,
   And spare the golden bindings!
              —*Robert Burns*

The Small Silver-Coloured Bookworm

Insatiate brute, whose teeth abuse
The sweetest servants of the muse!
His roses nipt in every page,
My poor Anacreon mourns thy rage;
By thee my Ovid wounded lies;
By thee my Lesbia's sparrow dies;
Thy rabid teeth have half destroy'd
The work of love in Biddy Floyd;
They rent Belinda's locks away,
And spoil'd the Blouzelind of Gay;
For all, for every single deed,
Relentless justice bids thee bleed.

Then fall a victim to the Nine,
Myself the priest, my desk the shrine.
—*Thomas Parnell*

Inchworm

The tiny inchworm's so supple it
'S easily fitted in a couplet.
—*D. A Prince*

For a Praying Mantis, Standing in the Need of Prayer

(The female praying mantis consumes her mate in the process of copulation.)

The Male (or Lesser) Praying Mantis is
A victim of romantic fantasies.
He cries, "My angel, let me prove
A mantis' life well lost for love!"
He takes her in his tender arms;
He soothes her virginal alarms—
Pours all his love and longing in her,

While she is having him for dinner.
He reassures her that they'll wed;
Meanwhile, she's gnawing off his head.
He soothes her gastric pains with Borax,
As she is working on his thorax;
And when there's nothing left above,
Still doth the Lower Mantis love.

This system, as needs scarcely saying,
Makes little Mantises . . . all praying.
                    —*Willard Espy*

Mantis

The praying mantis doesn't pray;
He simply likes to pose that way.
The sect which he's an insect in
Leads with its left and not the chin.
                    —*David McCord*

Triolet

I wish I were a jelly fish
That cannot fall downstairs:
Of all the things I wish to wish
I wish I were a jelly fish
That hasn't any cares,
And doesn't even have to wish
"I wish I were a jelly fish
That cannot fall downstairs."

—G. K. Chesterton

The Dolphin

Behold the ocean's gadabout—
   The frisky, friendly dolphin;
His head displays a smiling snout;
   His backside sports a tall fin;
Content to frolic in the sea,
   He's never fierce or warlike;
How happier our world would be
   If dolphins we were more like.

—Frank Jacobs

The Snake and Its Critics

The snake having caught
an excellent mouse
will not hunt again for a month

though the farmer whose wheat
the mouse has eaten
says why not catch more

though the mouse
dissolving in the long corridor
says no no already

you have caught
one mouse too many.
The snake however refuses

all such importunities
and gulps and curls and sleeps
as it pleases

doing neither great good
nor great evil but constantly
as little harm as possible.

—*Bonnie Jacobson*

If You Should Meet a Crocodile

If you should meet a Crocodile
    Don't take a stick and poke him;
Ignore the welcome in his smile,
    Be careful not to stroke him.
For as he sleeps upon the Nile,
    He thinner gets and thinner;
And whene'er you meet a Crocodile
    He's ready for his dinner.

          —Anonymous

The Birds of 9th Ave.

The birds of 9th Ave.
Look toward 3d Ave.
And see the new day coming
Long before I want to know about it.
They hail it en route
And pierce my slumber.
"Pipe down," I want to say,
"It's no big deal.
It'll come whether or not you greet it."

But then, clinging to the night
I doze off, thinking
If I were a 9th Ave. bird
With not much else to do
 I'd face the East
 And at the first peep of dawn
 I'd holler, too.

     —*Alma Denny*

The Bird

I love to hear the little bird
Into song by morning stirred,
Provided that he doesn't sing
Before my own awakening.
A bird that wakes a fellow up,
Should have been a buttercup.

    —*Samuel Hoffenstein*

Magpie Song

The magpie! The magpie! Here underneath
In the white of his wings are the footsteps of
    morning.
It dawns! It dawns!

        —*Anonymous*
        (Navajo Song
translated by Alice Cunningham Fletcher)

Hummingbird

A Route of Evanescence
With a revolving Wheel—
A Resonance of Emerald—
A Rush of Cochineal—
And every Blossom on the Bush
Adjusts its tumbled Head—
The mail from Tunis, probably,
An easy Morning's Ride—

        —*Emily Dickinson*

The Humming-Bird

What a boom! boom!
  Sounds among the honeysuckles!
Saying, "Room! room!
  Hold your breath and mind your knuckles!"
And a fairy birdling bright
Flits like a living dart of light,
With his tiny whirlwind wings
Flies and rests and sings.
All his soul one flash, one quiver,
  Down each cup
He thrusts his long beak with a shiver,
  Drinks the sweetness up;
Takes the best of earth and goes—
  Daring sprite!—
Back to his heaven no mortal knows,
A heaven as sweet as the heart of a rose
  Shut at night.

—*Harriet Monroe*

Cuckoo

Cuckoo, Cuckoo,
What do you do?

In April
I open my bill.

In May
I sing night and day.

In June
I change my tune.

In July
Away I fly.

In August,
Go I must.
—*Anonymous*

The Cuckoo

In April the Cuckoo can sing her song by rote,
In June out of tune she cannot sing a note.
At first, cuckoo, cuckoo, sing still she can do,
At last, cuc, cuc, cuc, six cucs to one koo.

—*John Heywood*

Cassowary

If I were a Cassowary
On the plains of Timbuctoo,
I would eat a missionary,
Cassock, band, and hymn-book too.

—*Samuel Wilberforce*

The Rabbit

The rabbit has a charming face;
Its private life is a disgrace.
I really dare not name to you
The awful things that rabbits do;

Things that your paper never prints—
You only mention them in hints.
They have such lost, degraded souls
No wonder they inhabit holes;
When such depravity is found
It can only live underground.

—*Anonymous*

Space Cat

Pusskin the Russian space-cat
on the end of a taut fee-line
the Meowscow circus ravelled out
from the space shuttle Cataline.

Did she research atoms from space
or a moon to Jupiter skitter?
No, only directions on how to manage
with weightless kitty litter.

—*Andrew Glaze*

Pillows

I love the ladies with cats on their laps,
The languorous ladies with cats on their laps,
Who seem to be listening twice to what you say,
And fondling, fondling, would never get up and
    walk away.

Not even if Pavarotti were singing.
Not even if the telephone were ringing.
Not even if you were rude, or cried.
Not even if the cat died.

—Bonnie Jacobson

The Kilkenny Cats

There wanst was two cats at Kilkenny,
Each thought there was one cat too many,
    So they quarrell'd and fit,
    They scratch'd and they bit,
    Till, excepting their nails,
    And the tips of their tails,
Instead of two cats, there warn't any.

—Anonymous

The Diners in the Kitchen

Our dog Fred
Et the bread.

Our dog Dash
Et the hash.

Our dog Pete
Et the meat.

Our dog Davy
Et the gravy.

Our dog Toffy
Et the coffee.

Our dog Jake
Et the cake.

Our dog Trip
Et the dip.

And the worst,
From the first,—

Our dog Fido
Et the pie-dough.
—*James Whitcomb Riley*

As I Went to Bonner

As I went to Bonner,
    I met a pig
    Without a wig,
Upon my word and honour.
    —*Anonymous*

As I Looked Out

As I looked out on Saturday last,
A fat little pig went hurrying past.
Over his shoulders he wore a shawl,
Although it didn't seem cold at all.
I waved at him, but he didn't see,
For he never so much as looked at me.
Once again, when the moon was high,
I saw the little pig hurrying by;
Back he came at a terrible pace,

The moonlight shone on his little pink face,
And he smiled with a smile that was quite content.
But never I knew where that little pig went.

—*Anonymous*

To a Pig

Bards and sages, through the ages
(Winning fame instead of wages),
Have mussed up a million pages
    With their outcries, small and big,
Singing wrongs that should be righted,
Causes blighted, heroes slighted—
Yet no song have they indited
        To the Pig.

Gentle Porcus, suoid mammal,
Does the thought that lard and ham'll
Be your future never trammel
    Your fond fancies as you dig?
Does it harrow to the marrow,
As you pace your quarters narrow,
Dreaming of the storied glory
        Of the Pig?

For time was, ere man got at you,
Using squalid means to fat you,
That you were to be congratu-
    Lated on a figure trig;
And most daintily you ate your
Food, less mingled in its nature;
Fine of face, full fair and graceful
      Was the Pig.

Oh, SPCA, be gracious;
If your sympathies be spacious,
Bar such treatment contumacious—
    Teach that it is infra dig;
For although some genius flighty
Has described the pen as mighty
You'll admit a sward were fitter
      For the Pig.

        —*Burgess Johnson*

Why Pigs Cannot Write Poems

Pigs cannot write poems because
Nothing rhymes with *oink*. If you
Think you can find a rhyme, I'll pause,

But if I wait until you do,
I'll have forgotten why it was
Pigs cannot write poems because.
—*John Ciardi*

The Smile of the Walrus

The Smile of the Walrus is wild and distraught,
    And tinged with pale purples and greens,
Like the Smile of a Thinker who thinks a Great
    Thought
    And isn't quite sure what it means.
—*Oliver Herford*

The Smile of the Goat

The Smile of the Goat has a meaning that few
    Will mistake, and explains in a measure
The Censor attending a risqué Revue
    And combining Stern Duty with pleasure.
—*Oliver Herford*

The Lama

The one-l lama
He's a priest.
The two-l llama,
He's a beast.
And I will bet
A silk pajama
There isn't any
Three-l lllama.

—*Ogden Nash*

A Llyric of the Llama

Behold how from her lair the youthful llama
   Llopes forth and llightly scans the llandscape o'er.
With llusty heart she llooks upon llife's drama,
   Relying on her llate-llearnt worldly llore.

But llo! Some llad, armed with a yoke *infama*
   Soon llures her into llowly llabor's cause;
Her wool is llopped to weave into pajama,
   And llanguidly she llearns her Gees and Haws.

My children, heed this llesson from all
    llanguishing young lllamas,
  If you would lllive with lllatitude, avoid each
    llluring lllay:
And do not llllightly lllleave, I beg, your llllonesome,
    lllloving mammas,
  And llllast of allll, don't spelllll your name in such
    a sillllllly way.

—*Burgess Johnson*

The Purple Cow

I never saw a Purple Cow,
I never hope to see one;
But I can tell you, anyhow,
I'd rather see than be one.

—*Gelett Burgess*

Cinq Ans Après

Ah, yes! I wrote the "Purple Cow"—
I'm Sorry, now, I Wrote it!
    But I can Tell you, Anyhow,
    I'll Kill you if you Quote it!
          —Gelett Burgess

The Horse

I know two things about the horse,
And one of them is rather coarse.
          —Anonymous

The Gnu

G stands for Gnu, whose weapons of defense
Are long, sharp, curling horns, and common sense.
To these he adds a name so short and strong,
That even hardy Boers pronounce it wrong.
How often on a bright autumnal day
The pious people of Pretoria say

"Come, let us hunt the———" then no more is
    heard,
But sounds of strong men struggling with a word;
Meanwhile the distant Gnu with grateful eyes
Observes his opportunity and flies.

—*Hilaire Belloc*

Have You Ever Been Near a Giraffe

Have you ever been near a giraffe
When he's having a very good laugh?
        It starts, you will note,
        At the top of his throat,
And lasts for an hour and a half.

—*Laurence Perrine*

Have Crate, Will Travel

A much-traveled hippo
Residing in Looe
Is the toast of the town
And deserves to be, too.

In plush hippo crates,
He is sent to meet mates
In such faraway places
As Lima, Peru.

—*Bruce E. Newling*

The Song of Hippopotamus

All day the hippopotami
Deep in the languid waters lie
Which sometimes gently stir and seethe
When they lift up their heads to breathe.

Together thus the he and she
Restore themselves to energy
Until the blood begins to move
With massive pulse of mammoth love.

Then how the waters crash and churn!
Unquenchable, the hippos burn
With every passion of their kind
In boundless flesh and fervent mind

Till, echoing for miles around,
Their natural, ecstatic sound

Inspires an answering refrain
From every creature on the plain.

O love, as languidly we lie
Late in our bed, warm thigh to thigh,
And slowly wake, there thrills through us
The Song of Hippopotamus!
                —*Barbara K. Loots*

FOUR

Jabberwocky, or
verbal fun & sheer nonsense

Jabberwocky

'Twas brillig, and the slithy toves
   Did gyre and gimble in the wabe;
All mimsy were the borogoves,
   and the mome raths outgrabe.

"Beware the Jabberwock, my son!
   The jaws that bite, the claws that catch!
Beware the Jubjub bird, and shun
   The frumious Bandersnatch!"

He took his vorpal sword in hand;
   Long time the manxome foe he sought—
So rested he by the Tumtum tree,
   And stood awhile in thought.

And as in uffish thought he stood,
   The Jabberwock, with eyes of flame,
Came whiffling through the tulgey wood,
   And burbled as it came!

One, two! One, two! And through and through
   The vorpal blade went snicker-snack!
He left it dead, and with its head
   He went galumphing back.

"And hast thou slain the Jabberwock?
    Come to my arms, my beamish boy!
O frabjous day! Callooh! Callay!"
    He chortled in his joy.

'Twas brillig, and the slithy toves
    Did gyre and gimble in the wabe;
All mimsy were the borogoves,
    And the mome raths outgrabe.
                    —*Lewis Carroll*

Hollywood Jabberwocky

'Twas Bogart and the Franchot Tones
    Did Greer and Garson in the Wayne;
All Muni were the Lewis Stones,
    And Rooneyed with Fontaine.

"Beware the deadly Rathbone, son!
    Don't Bellamy the Barrymore!
Beware that you the Greenstreet shun,
    And likewise Eric Blore!"

He took his Oakie firm in hand,
    Long time the Bracken foe to quell;
He stopped to pray at Turhan Bey,
    And murmured, "Joan Blondell."

And as he Breened with Jagger drawn,
    The deadly Rathbone, eyes Astaire,
Came Rafting through the Oberon
    And Harlowed everywhere!

Sabu! Sabu! And Richard Loo!
    The Oakie gave a Hardwicke smack!
He seized its Flynn, and with a Quinn,
    He went Karloffing back.

"And didst thou Dunne the Rathbone, Ladd?
    Come Grable in the Eddy, boy!
O Alice Faye! O Joel McCrea!"
    He Cagneyed in his Loy.

'Twas Bogart and the Franchot Tones
    Did Greer and Garson in the Wayne;
All Muni were the Lewis Stones,
    And Rooneyed with Fontaine.
                            —*Frank Jacobs*

One Old Oxford Ox

One old Oxford ox opening oysters;
Two tee-totums totally tired of trying to trot to
    Tadbury;
Three tall tigers tippling tenpenny tea;
Four fat friars fanning fainting flies;
Five frippy Frenchmen foolishly fishing for flies;
Six sportsmen shooting snipes;
Seven Severn salmons swallowing shrimps;
Eight Englishmen eagerly examining Europe;
Nine nimble noblemen nibbling nonpareils;
Ten tinkers tinkling upon ten tin tinder-boxes with
    ten tenpenny tacks;
Eleven elephants elegantly equipt;
Twelve typographical typographers typically
    translating types.

—*Anonymous*

I Missed His Book,
But I Read His Name

"The Silver Pilgrimage," by M. Anantanarayanan.
. . . 160 pages. Criterion. $3.95.

—*The Times*

Though authors are a dreadful clan
To be avoided if you can,
I'd like to meet the Indian,
M. Anantanarayanan.

I picture him as short and tan.
We'd meet, perhaps, in Hindustan.
I'd say, with admirable *élan*,
"Ah, Anantanarayanan—

I've heard of you. The *Times* once ran
A notice on your novel, an
Unusual tale of God and Man."
And Anantanarayanan

Would seat me on a lush divan
And read his name—that sumptuous span
Of "a's" and "n's" more lovely than
"In Xanadu did Kubla Khan"—

Aloud to me all day. I plan
Henceforth to be an ardent fan
Of Anantanarayanan—
M. Anantanarayanan.

—*John Updike*

Sonnet from the Brooklynese

My heart is gayly purzed as if it wuy
   Ra buyd about to dart in jeryous flight
   To you; my darling, may it but alight
On vuygin surl. And may it not incuy
Your anger or disdain. 'Tis but a fleuy
   D'amour, and if you spuyn it you will blight
   Its life as if some purzon in the night
Had been instilled into its depths. You stuy

My soul into a tuymurl. If you've turyed
With me, I fain would hie me to a clurster,
   Wherein my heart would never be annuryed
By thoughts of love. My eyes grow murst and
     murster
   At contemplating such an aching vurd—
O grant me, then, the sang-froid of an urster.

—*Margaret Fishback*

I Once Had a Schoolmate Named Cholomondeley*

I once had a schoolmate named Cholomondeley.
He bore his name proudly but holomondeley.
　　His friends liked him well,
　　But they sent him no mail
Lest their spelling be seen as uncolomondeley.

—*Laurence Perrine*

*pronounced *Chumley*

In Lodium

Podium is simply a form of *pew.*
　　　　—*A TV quiz*

They said it was a podium,
　　A podium or pew;
A thing I never knodium,
　　I never, never knew.
Which controversial vodium
　　Or questionable view,
Intelligence must rodium,
　　Must rodium or rue;

And treat with scornful odium,
Or take with grain of sodium,
With grains of chloride sodium,
And not of these a fodium,
    A fodium or few.

    —*Anonymous*

When Ounce Is Spelled Oz.

A girl who weighed many an oz.
Used language I dare not pronoz.
    When a fellow unkind
    Pulled her chair out behind
Just to see (so he said) if she'd boz.

    —*Anonymous*

The Poet Sings the Passing of His Love

When Zoe's shop was simply labelled LUNCHES,
I used to send her flowers in great big bunches.
But when she changed it to YE LUNCHEON SHOPPE,
I sent her one symbolic final poppe.

—*Richard Usborne*

A Man Hired by John Smith and Co.*

A man hired by John Smith and Co.
Loudly declared he would tho.
    Man that he saw
    Dumping dirt near his store.
The drivers, therefore, didn't do.

—*Mark Twain*

* pronounced *company*

How Much Did Philadelphia Pa?

How much did Philadelphia Pa?
  Whose grass did K.C. Mo?
How many eggs could New Orleans La?
  How much does Cleveland O?

When Hartford and New Haven Conn
  What sucker do they soak?
Could Noah build a Little Rock Ark
  If he had not Guthrie Ok?

We call Minneapolis Minn,
  Why not Annapolis Ann?
If you can't tell the reason why
  I'll bet Topeka Kan.

But now we speak of ladies, what
  A Butte Montana is!
If I could borrow Memphis' Tenn
  I'd treat that Jackson Miss.

Would Denver Cola cop because
  Ottumwa Ia dore?
Ah, though my Portland Me doth love,
  I threw my Portland Ore.

—*Anonymous*

I Saw a Fishpond

I saw a fishpond all on fire
I saw a house bow to a squire
I saw a parson twelve feet high
I saw a cottage near the sky
I saw a balloon made of lead
I saw a coffin drop down dead
I saw two sparrows run a race
I saw two horses making lace
I saw a girl just like a cat
I saw a kitten wear a hat
I saw a man who saw these too
And said though strange they were all true.

—*Anonymous*

Note: This verse makes perfect sense if the reader supplies appropriate punctuation: "I saw a fishpond." "All on fire I saw a house." etc.

Local Note

In Sparkill buried lies that man of mark
Who brought the Obelisk to Central Park,
Redoubtable Commander H. H. Gorringe,
Whose name supplies the long-sought rhyme for
    "orange."

        —*Arthur Guiterman*

Attention!

All hail the generalissimo
Who pressed his pants prestissimo
Scaled the fort fortissimo
Braved the fray bravissimo
And rang the bells bellissimo.
All hail the generalissimo!

        —*Jane Gilliat Fry*

A Tooter Who Tooted the Flute

A tutor who tooted the flute
Tried to tutor two tooters to toot.
Said the two to the tutor,
"Is it harder to toot or
To tutor two tooters to toot?"
—*Carolyn Wells*

There Was an Old Lady of Ryde

There was an old lady of Ryde
Who ate some green apples, and died.
The apples (fermented
Inside the lamented)
Made cider inside 'er inside.
—*Anonymous*

A Parody of "Hiawatha"

He had mittens, Minjekahwun,
Buckskin mittens made of deerskin;
Mittens with the fur-side outside,
Mittens with the skin-side inside.
When he turned them inside outside,
When he turned them outside inside,
Then the warm side, fur-side, in was,
And the cold side, skin-side, out was;
When he turned them outside inside,
When he turned them inside outside.

—*George A. Strong*

The Bottle of Perfume
That Willie Sent

The bottle of perfume that Willie sent
Was highly displeasing to Millicent.
   Her thanks were so cold
   That they quarreled, I'm told,
Through that silly scent Willie sent Millicent.

—*Anonymous*

For Bears

Four bears of their forebears were proud,
Four pairs were their parents—allowed.
   But those, besides claws,
      Had *their* paws and *their* maws . . .
One forbears to list the whole crowd.

—*Laurence Perrine*

Epitaph

Beneath these high Cathedral stairs
Lie the remains of Susan Pares.
Her name was Wiggs, it was not Pares,
But Pares was put to rhyme with stairs.

—*Edward Lear*

History of Education

The decent docent doesn't doze:
He teaches standing on his toes.

His student dassn't doze—and does,
And that's what teaching is and was.
—*David McCord*

Unnecessary Punishments

Atlas grunted, shouldering the globe:
"Jesus! This is a job for Job!"
—*William Cole*

How to Pronounce
My Last Name

Man, matron, maiden,
Please call it Baden;
Further for Powell,
Rhyme it with Noel.
—*Robert Baden-Powell*

Mr. Punchinello

Oh! mother, I shall be married to Mr. Punchinello.
>To Mr. Punch,
>To Mr. Joe,
>To Mr. Nell,
>To Mr. Lo,
>Mr. Punch, Mr. Joe,
>Mr. Nell, Mr. Lo,
>To Mr. Punchinello.

>>*—Anonymous*

To Madame X
with a Brace of Duck

I've dispatch'd, my dear madam, this scrap of a
    letter,
To say that Miss—— is very much better.
A Regular Doctor no longer she lacks.
And therefore I've sent her a couple of Quacks.

>>*—Dr. Edward Jenner*

A World War II Nose

My nose, my nose lived dangerously
    Its courage was no stunt!
And during the war in Germany
    It was always out in front!

Yet when the battle was o'er
    And we'd defeated the Hun
Suddenly, for no reason at all
    My nose started to run.
                  —Spike Milligan

Untitled

This poem's title is Untitled—
Not because it is untitled,
But because I am entitled
To entitle it Untitled.

If I'd not titled it Untitled,
It would truly be untitled . . .
Which would make me unentitled
To entitle it Untitled.

So it is vital, if untitled,
Not to title it Untitled,
And to leave that title idled,
As a title is entitled.
—*Kenneth Leonhardt*

The Elevator Operator–
Operated Elevator

When you sin, friend, know that later
You'll meet Charon, operator
Of an ancient elevator.
   It goes down to Hades' crater;
It goes up to your Creator.
Charon sets the indicator.
     Ponder well that antiquated
     Manually operated
   Elevator operator–
   Operated elevator.
       —*Willard Espy*

The Boy

Down through the snow-drifts in the street
  With blustering joy he steers;
His rubber boots are full of feet
  And his tippet full of ears.

        —Eugene Field

Amo, Amas

Amo, amas
I loved a lass
  Ah me, but she was tender!
Amas, amat
She left me flat
  I hate the feminine gender.

        —Anonymous

A Latin Little Jack Horner

Parvus Jacobus Horner
Sedebat in corner,
Edens a Christmas pie;

Inferit thumb,
Extraherit plum—
Clamans, "Quid sharp puer am I!"
—*Anonymous*

A Latin Little Bo-Peep

Parvula Bo-Peep
Amisit her sheep,
Et nescit where to find 'em;
Desere alone,
Et venient home,
Cum omnibus caudis behind 'em.

—*Anonymous*

The Despondee's Lament

Drip-drop!   Plip-plop!
Damned rain won't stop.
Wind, rain, streaked pane,
Splish-splosh down lane.

Dogs growl, cats howl,
Roof leaks, feel foul.
Cough-cough! Don't scoff—
Bad cold; ticked off.

Wind's dropped; rain's stopped;
Mood's changed—flip-flopped.
              —*Bruce E. Newling*

from *Celebrations & Bewilderments*

"They were learning to draw," the Dormouse went
on, yawning and rubbing its eyes, for it was getting very
sleepy; "and they drew all manner of things—everything that begins with an M—"

"Why with an M?" said Alice.

"Why not?" said the March Hare.

              —*Lewis Carroll*

My muse makes merry,
Much music
Made mirthful,
Moon-mad.
More, more, more,

More mischief.
My mien
Mirrors
My moods,
My mind,
My manners,
Metered motion,
My muse makes melody.

Metaphor mends me,
My mad medley,
Man-matrixed.
Matter mold me,
Mouth mysteries,
Mute miracles.
Mountebank, mourn me,
My measured masque.
My muse moves me.
My metaphor mends me.
      —*Louis Phillips*

FIVE

A Bit of Americana,
meaning baseball, automobiles, advertising, & almost everything else

Boston

I come from the city of Boston,
   The home of the bean and the cod,
Where Cabots speak only to Lowells,
   And Lowells speak only to God.

          —Samuel C. Bushnell

Revised

Then here's to the City of Boston,
   The town of the cries and the groans,
Where the Cabots can't see the Kabotschniks,
   And the Cabots won't speak to the Cohns.

          —Franklin P. Adams

The Boston Evening Transcript

The readers of the *Boston Evening Transcript*
Sway in the wind like a field of ripe corn.

When evening quickens faintly in the street,
Wakening the appetites of life in some

And to others bringing the *Boston Evening
        Transcript,*
I mount the steps and ring the bell, turning
Wearily, as one would turn to nod good-bye to
        Rochefoucauld,
If the street were time and he at the end of the
        street,
And I say, "Cousin Harriet, here is the *Boston
        Evening Transcript.*"

—*T. S. Eliot*

New Yorkers

Everywhere else in the country, if someone asks,
How are you?, you are required to answer,
like a phrase book, Fine, and you?

Only in New York can you say, Not so good, or
        even,
Rotten, and launch into your miseries and
        symptoms,
then yawn and look bored when they interrupt
to go into endless detail about their own.

Nodding mechanically, you look at your watch.
Look, angel, I've got to run, I'm late for my . . .
    uh . . .
uh . . . analyst. But let's definitely
get together soon.

In just as sincere a voice as yours,
they come back with, Definitely!
and both of you know what that means,
Never.

                            —*Edward Field*

Manhattan Lullabye

Hush, my little baby,
    Before you go to sleep,
Listen to the lullabye
    Of BEEP, BEEP, BEEP,

Honk, whirr, HONK, HONK,
    Clomp, BANG, bang, crash,
"Watch where yer goin', Mac!"
    Clomp, bang, BANG, smash!

VAROOM, varooom, pa-tow,
  Buzz, Woooo-wooo, Careee.
Forget it, Kid, you might as well
  Stay up all night with me.
        —*Louis Phillips*

Times-Square-Shoeshine-Composition

I'm the best that ever done it
(pow pow)
    that's my title and I won it
    (pow pow)
I ain't lying, I'm the best
(pow pow)
    Come and put me to the test
    (pow pow)

I'll clean 'em til they squeak
(pow pow)
    In the middle of next week,
    (pow pow)
I'll shine 'em til they whine
(pow pow)

Till they call me master mine
(pow pow)

For a quarter and a dime
(pow pow)
    You can get the dee luxe shine
    (pow pow)
Say you wanta pay a quarter?
(pow pow)
    Then you give that to your daughter
    (pow pow)

I ain't playing dozens mister
(pow pow)
    You can give it to your sister
    (pow pow)
Any way you want to read it
(pow pow)
    Maybe it's your momma need it.
    (pow pow)

Say I'm like a greedy bigot,
(pow pow)
    I'm a cap'tilist, can you dig it?
    (pow pow)
          —Maya Angelou

Aubade: *NYC*

it is morning darling look the sun
by the fire escape comes peeping
rose on our sheets how fresh how
still oh and the roaches are sleeping
—*Robert Wallace*

The Devil in Texas

He scattered tarantulas over the roads,
Put thorns on the cactus and horns on the toads,
He sprinkled the sands with millions of ants
So the man who sits down must wear soles on his
    pants.
He lengthened the horns of the Texas steer,
And added an inch to the jack rabbit's ear;
He put mouths full of teeth in all of the lakes,
And under the rocks he put rattlesnakes.

He hung thorns and brambles on all of the trees,
He mixed up the dust with jiggers and fleas;
The rattlesnake bites you, the scorpion stings,
The mosquito delights you by buzzing his wings.

The heat in the summer's a hundred and ten,
Too hot for the Devil and too hot for men;
And all who remain in that climate soon bear
Cuts, bites, and stings, from their feet to their hair.

He quickened the buck of the bronco steed,
And poisoned the feet of the centipede;
The wild boar roams in the black chaparral;
It's a hell of a place that we've got for a hell.
He planted red pepper beside every brook;
The Mexicans use them in all that they cook.
Just dine with a Mexican, then you will shout,
"I've hell on the inside as well as the out!"

—*Anonymous*

The Midwest

Across those plains
Where once there roamed
  The Indian and the Scout,
The Swede
With alcoholic breath
  Sets rows of cabbage out.

—*Anonymous*

The New Reconstruction

Are they really Southern, those glossy magazines
with "South" or "Southern" in their titles?
It's carpetbagging in reverse:
full of ads for resorts we don't visit,
festivals and craft fairs we don't attend:
cornbread recipes for those who don't know how.
And when they run out of cornbread recipes,
who knows what they'll try next?
Southern quiche, maybe: instant cheese grits
stirred into scrambled eggs; or maybe
black-eyed peas and okra marinade.
God help 'em, though, if they try sushi—
down here raw fish is bait.

                                        —*David Black*

The Philadelphia Maid

My family have all been saints
    For twenty generations,
Quite free from all the tints and taints
    Of worldly dissipations.

All pleasure they consider crime;
    Of love they were not makers;
They never went out for "a time,"
    For all of them were Quakers.
Emotion I have never felt;
    It was against the law;
For I was born and always dwelt
    In Phil-a-del-phi-a.

O 'tis a place of solemn lives,
    Where joy has never tarried;
There husbands may not kiss their wives
    Till they've been two years married.
There William Penn his vigil keeps;
    With reverence I name him.
'Tis there that old Ben Franklin sleeps—
    For which no one can blame him.
It takes a hundred years for one
    To be a grandmamma.
No clocks are fast; no watches run
    In Phil-a-del-phi-a.

                    —*Harry B. Smith*

Traveling Through Louisiana
on One Shirt

Medea must have designed it out of spit
and spite. It was the first no-iron.
In motel rooms, I washed it every night
after a scorching day of sightseeing.

Next morning, it was dry and ready for
another Chrétien Point, Trepagnier, or Parlange.
It could have lined cracker boxes or
cookie tins. It kept crisp, didn't breathe. Even gnats

and mosquitoes couldn't penetrate. It ballooned
at the waist and shoulders. It restorethed
my goal of seeing all the old plantation
houses in Louisiana, that, wrapped in a shirt

like this, would never have crumbled
picturesquely out of their Greek Revival,
Gothic, or West Indian architectural modes.
Even when we opened the shuttered portal

of Belle Hélène, ignoring the posted No
Trespassing sign, it would have warded off
buckshot and deputy sheriffs. It was not bio-

degradable. It absolutely outlawed and double-
     crossed

each crease and wrinkle. It was sweat-
resistant, though I was not. I parboiled
under that synthesis of sun and manufactured
cloth some bright, accursed, upwardly mobile

minion had devised in a frenzied spell of so-called
genius. I reviled him by day. I blessed
him at night. On weedy footpaths and byroads
of history and dust, in dim and noon-hushed

allées of live oaks, the aerial moss
of one parasitic witchcraft of shirt
wove an indestructible dimension, timeless
and fraught, into an unalterable future and past.

So I salute it, flag of my own discovery.
Long may it wave (and I know it still does)
over confederacies of dream-states and colonies,
ever determinedly brave, defiantly free—

the wash-and-wear pre-shrink of lucent mesh,
the drip-dry Creole of fact and fantasy.
                    —*Marvin Solomon*

Pledge for the
Loyal Temperance Union,
1883

I promise not to buy, sell or give
Alcoholic liquors while I live;
From all tobacco I'll abstain
And never take God's name in vain.

—*Frances E. Willard*

Antoine de Cadillac

Higgledy-piggledy
Antoine de Cadillac
Founded Detroit and did
Nothing else much.

Still there's his name on an
Octocylindrical
Car like a Lincoln or
Chrysler or such.

—*Anthony Harrington*

Mourning Becomes Eugene O'Neill

Eugene G. O'Neill
  Moans a great, great deal.
Eugene G. O'Neill
  Disrupts the evening meal.
Eugene G. O'Neill,
  Tart as lemon peel,
  Sad as cold boiled veal,
  Weighing woe and weal,
  What anguish must he feel!
Eugene G. O'Neill,
  Slightly off his keel
  With sombre, Freudian zeal,
  Makes the blood congeal,
  The senses reel.
Eugene G. O'Neill
  Probes with bitter steel
  Wounds that none may heal.
Three ouches and a squeal
  For Eugene G. O'Neill!
          —Arthur Guiterman

Parable

Re: "Elmer Gantry"

A redheaded woodpecker tries to tackle
The tin roof of the tabernacle.
The din is great but the damage small;
That's "Red" Lewis, after all.

—*Keith Preston*

The Folk Ballad of Neil Armstrong

When he was a boy, Neil Armstrong dreamed
  He was floating and could not land.
He skimmed, and he hovered, and he cried out
    loud,
  "Please, please let me understand!"

He lived in a house by a buckeye tree
  And rousted about in its deep dark shade.
He rode his bike down Ohio roads
  And fished in rivers green as jade.

But then he grew up and he took a ship
   All the way to the moon.
Buzz and Michael were there with him
   And Neil would be landing soon.

The moon looked dead as a ghost's pale face
   You might see in a haunted pool.
"Come," said the moon, "come down to me,
   If you are a fool, a fool."

"I'll come," said Neil, "I'll come to you,
   Down to your cratered face.
I'll come or I'll die. I can't go back.
   I'm tired of living in space."

And Earth was a long, long ways away,
   A marble of white and blue
Where clouds rolled on and oceans tossed
   And dreams came sometimes true.

The rockets roared and the numbers flared;
   Neil dropped to the moon's white lip.
"Go back," said the moon. "Go back, go back,
   You'll die in the crash of your ship."

"I ride the Eagle," Neil's voice sang.
   "I ride the Eagle to you."

Alarm bells rang and voices screamed,
  The dust cloud blew and blew.

"Houston, Houston, help me out.
  I miss the sea and sky.
If I can't find a place to land,
  I think that I will die."

The lights went on and the legs stood still.
  The engine arm went off.
A billion people wept and cheered
  Upon the watching Earth.

And in his suit of white, Neil spoke
  The words you have in mind.
"That's one small step for man," he said,
  "A giant leap for mankind."

And Michael, in the mother ship,
  And Buzz who stood beside,
Were silent as two fishermen
  Who watch the rising tide.

Oh Earthlings, Earthlings, don't forget
  That once he walked up there,
And looking down on us, he thought,
  How beautiful and fair.

How beautiful the rolling clouds,
How lovely to splash in the foam,
But lovelier still is the buckeye tree
Of my Ohio home.

—*Dick Allen*

Uncalled-for Epitaph

W. R.*

I worked with gum and grin and lariat
To entertain the proletariat,
And with my Oklahomely wit
I brightened up the earth a bit.
I'd brighten Heaven with my capers—
But shucks, the Lord don't read the papers.

—*Ogden Nash*

*Will Rogers

Insult Is the Soul of Wit

Groucho Marx is a man I'm fond of.
A gray-haired jest he can make a blonde of.
But I'd rather be a derelict, sleeping in parks,
Than a guest on the program of Groucho Marx.

—*Phyllis McGinley*

General Custer

General Custer rode with pride.
The lust for battle filled him.
Hell-bent was he on Siouxicide—
And, sure enough, it killed him.

—*Bob McKenty*

The Ballad of Lizzie Borden

Lizzie Borden took an ax,
Gave her mother forty whacks;
When she saw what she had done,
Gave her father forty-one.

—*Anonymous*

Andrew Jackson

Andrew Jackson
Was an Anglo-Saxon
Who lived on pork and beans.
When tired of that,
he lived on fat,
Hog-jowls and greens.

—*Anonymous*

Elinor Glyn

Would you like to sin
With Eleanor Glyn
On a tiger-skin?
Or would you prefer
to err
with her
on some other fur?

—*Anonymous*

John Wesley Gaines

John Wesley Gaines!
John Wesley Gaines!
Thou monumental mass of brains!
Come in, John Wesley
For it rains.

—Anonymous

Ole Man Dan was a
Tough Ole Man

Ole Man Dan was a tough ole man,
Washed his face in the fryin' pan;
Combed his hair with a wagon wheel,
Died with a toothache in his heel.

—Anonymous

The Banjo Player

There is music in me, the music of a peasant
    people.
I wander through the levee, picking my banjo and
    singing my songs of the cabin and the field.
At the Last Chance Saloon I am as welcome as
    the violets in March; there is always food and
    drink for me there, and the dimes of those
    who love honest music. Behind the railroad
    tracks the little children clap their hands and
    love me as they love Kris Kringle.
But I fear that I am a failure.
    Last night a woman called me a troubadour.
What is a troubadour?

—*Fenton Johnson*

A Wail from a Pulpeteer

If I could end this servitude
To need for coin, so gross and lewd,
I'd face the world with fortitude
    No doubt.

If I had four and twenty blonds
A diamond and a stack of bonds,
Some caviar, and beer in ponds
      I'd flout

Inferior scum who write for cash
Neglect their "art" and deal in trash,
And from my pen they'd feel the lash
      Of blame.

In pleasant comfort, quite content,
I'd sit secure—and scorn I'd vent
While they wrote tripe to pay the rent
      Of shame.

I'd lash those literary lice
With patronizing "good advice"
I'd wreck their pulpy paradise
      And write

Of "selling souls" and "prostitution"—
With violent words and elocution
I'd demand their bloody execution—
      The blight!

But all the phrases that I sculp
Are buried in some woody pulp

And as my weary sobs I gulp
         I try

To scratch out stories for my meat,
And just perhaps a Sunday treat
For Nature tells me I must eat—
         But Why?
             —*Louis L'Amour*

On Buying a Horse

One white foot, try him;
Two white feet, buy him;
Three white feet, put him in the dray;
Four white feet, give him away;
Four white feet, and a white nose,
Take off his hide and feed him to the crows.

             —*Anonymous*

Farmers Almanac

A swarm of bees in May
Is worth a load of hay;

A swarm of bees in June
Is worth a silver spoon;
A swarm of bees in July
Is not worth a fly.

—*Anonymous*

Waking Up in the Morning Thinking About Billy the Kid

Out of the blue it comes to me,
What Pat Garrett sd
About Billy the Kid,
That Billy "Drank and laughed,
Rode and laughed,
Talked and laughed,
Fought and laughed,
And killed and laughed."
Damn it!
Today's Tuesday.
That's exactly what I want to do.

—*Louis Phillips*

The Memoirs of Jesse James

I remember all those thousands of hours
that I spent in grade school watching the clock,
waiting for recess or lunch or to go home.
    Waiting: for anything but school.
My teachers could easily have ridden with Jesse
    James
    for all the time they stole from me.
              —*Richard Brautigan*

Late Registration

She asks me for an admissions card
to remedial English,
and I have to tell her that
we don't have any sections open.

"How come?" she asks.

So I explain that the governor provided
the money to identify those students
in need of remedial instruction,

but he did not budget any funds
for remedial instructors.

"Well, then," she says,
"put me down for creative writing."
—*Gerald Locklin*

The Base Stealer

Poised between going on and back, pulled
Both ways taut like a tightrope-walker,
Fingertips pointing the opposites,
Now bouncing tiptoe like a dropped ball
Or a kid skipping rope, come on, come on,
Running a scattering of steps sidewise,
How he teeters, skitters, tingles, teases,
Taunts them, hovers like an ecstatic bird,
He's only flirting, crowd him, crowd him,
Delicate, delicate, delicate, delicate—now!
—*Robert Francis*

Baseball's Sad Lexicon

These are the saddest of possible words:
    "Tinker to Evers to Chance."
Trio of bear cubs, and fleeter than birds,
    Tinker and Evers and Chance.
Ruthlessly pricking our gonfalon bubble,
Making a Giant hit into a double——
Words that are heavy with nothing but trouble:
    "Tinker to Evers to Chance."

                  —*Franklin P. Adams*

Residuals

Tom, his gun-colored coat raised,
slips on the slick kitchen floor and skids
SMACK into the refrigerator;

Just as Jerry—his legs a pinwheel of haze—
careens around the corner
(amidst a pack of hungry hounds)
and slides into an opportune mouse hole—gr-r-r-r!

And poor Tom, turning blue degree by degree,
wished to hell he hadn't read the rest of the script
that morning on the way to work.

—*Burnham Holmes*

Lone Ranger

An orange glow in the dark: the Masked Man
Is tied to the rails: and it is 1947.
I snuggle in the quilt. I am excellent at snuggling.
I am excellent at the sixtieth story window
All day long counting the cars of the world.
My mother points out the air-raid shades in the
    Museum of Natural History.
Soon after, she is trapped in the elevator.
My father breaks his nose in a car-crash.
I am the only kid on the block to be
Run over by a Good Humor truck.
This is: The Aftermath of World War II:
Running boards, pages of *Collier's* to cut out,
A world to cut up, out, and into,
My great, silver scissors.
An orange glow, and it is getting larger: specter
Of that shadowy massacre in the Panhandle,
The best blood of Texas seeping into the arroyos.

Masked Man, there is a sister born in the week of
    Hiroshima.
There is a Flexible Flyer and a small book about a
    bathtub tugboat,
Who is sent down the river to the ocean.
It is the William Tell Overture for the four
    hundredth time.
I lie there like a small corpse in cowboy pajamas.
I am something without feelings,
Without mind, without hair under the arms.
I am a lungfish in a gigantic bed.
The world is a ghost in a white sheet.
I am some creature in the year of the Marshall
    Plan
Hurtling across Lexington Avenue in a vortex of
    popsicles.

—*Thomas Frosch*

Advertising Advice

When your client's hopping mad,
Put his picture in the ad.
If he still should prove refractory
Add a picture of his factory.

—*Anonymous*

Burma-Shave Roadside Signs*

WITHIN THIS VALE
OF TOIL
AND SIN
YOUR HEAD GROWS BALD
BUT NOT YOUR CHIN—USE
BURMA-SHAVE

BE A MODERN
PAUL REVERE
SPREAD THE NEWS
FROM EAR
TO EAR
BURMA-SHAVE

THE QUEEN
OF HEARTS
NOW LOVES THE KNAVE
THE KING
RAN OUT OF
BURMA-SHAVE

NO LADY LIKES
TO DANCE
OR DINE
ACCOMPANIED BY
A PORCUPINE
BURMA-SHAVE

THE BURMA GIRLS
IN MANDALAY
DUNK BEARDED LOVERS
IN THE BAY
WHO DON'T USE
BURMA-SHAVE

MY JOB IS
KEEPING FACES CLEAN
AND NOBODY KNOWS
DE STUBBLE
I'VE SEEN
BURMA-SHAVE

*These roadside jingles, now a part of American folklore, were developed by advertising executive Allan G. Odell (1903–94).

Lydia Pinkham

Then we'll sing of Lydia Pinkham,
    And her love for the human race;
How she sold her veg'table compound
    And the papers publish'd her face.

Oh, it sells for a dollar a bottle
    Which is very cheap you see,
And if it doesn't cure you,
    She will sell you six for three.

              —Anonymous

Marble-Top

At counters where I eat my lunch
    In dim arcades of industry,
I cock my elbows up and munch
    Whatever food occurs to me.

By many mirrors multiplied,
    My silly face is not exalted;
And when I leave I have inside
    An egg-and-lettuce and a malted.

And just to hear the pretty peal
  Of merry maids at their pimento
Is more to me than any meal
  Or banquet that I ever went to.
      —*E. B. White*

Ode to an Elevator

Capricious, upsy-downsy sweet,
  My patience with thy presence crown!
Pray, when thy rising I entreat,
No more, dear love, rush past my feet
  Down!

Behold thy button burning bright,
  A signal thou wilt be here soon—
If not today, if not tonight,
Some other day, when clappers smite
  Noon.

I hear thee rising! Praise to thee,
  And praise to God, and praise to luck!—
Though well I know that presently,
'Twixt Six and Seven, I shall be
  Stuck.

Thy door slides open. Slightly squiffed,
   I sense too late the empty draft.
A lesser lover would be miffed
To find no life, but only lift
   Shaft.

I pray thee no salt tears to shed;
   I pray thee, drink no hemlock cup.
But I adjure thee, who am dead,
When next I press thy button, head
   Up.

                              —*Willard Espy*

For a Telephone Answering Machine

(with a thought from Catullus)

I speak, an empty room.
You speak now too! Entomb
your voice and what you mean
with mine in my machine.

Thus death, old lovers rave,
unites them in their grave,

clasping, still growing older,
still mixing as they molder.
—*Richard Moore*

Cellular

For blocks, the guy in the car ahead
has been talking on his phone.
If I had one and his line weren't busy,
I'd call to say the light turned green.
—*Robert Wallace*

Wild Boars and Lions Haul Admetus' Car

Wild boars and lions haul Admetus' car.
White horses seven serve the Morning Star.
A panther team takes Bacchus on his way,
While peacocks Juno's chariot convey.
By chastened lions Cybele is drawn,
And antlered stags bear fair Diana on.
Behind her wingèd dragons Ceres travels,

And flights of doves draw Venus to her revels.
Sea horses carry their thalassic Lord.
I drive a Ford.

—*Willard Espy*

Song of the Open Road

The Interstate goes mainly straight.
Sometimes around. Or up. Or down.

Woods pass by. Some barns and houses.
Fields with tractors, fields with cowses.

—*Robert Wallace*

Point of View

When Abraham Lincoln was murdered
The thing that interested Matthew Arnold
Was that the assassin
Shouted in Latin
As he leapt on the stage.
This convinced Matthew
There was still hope for America.

—*Christopher Morley*

SIX

Eat, Drink, & Be Merry,
or
a general celebration
of the seasons & good living

An Immorality

Sing we for love and idleness,
Naught else is worth the having.

Though I have been in many a land,
There is naught else in living.

And I would rather have my sweet,
Though rose-leaves die of grieving,

Than do high deeds in Hungary
To pass all men's believing.
—*Ezra Pound*

Spring

Spring comes again. I think that's nice.
    It is a season of which I'm fond.
Soon the beer bottles on the ice
    will disappear into the pond.
—*Richard Moore*

172

Spring Fjord

I was out in my kayak
I was out at sea in it
I was paddling
very gently in the fjord Ammassivik
there was ice in the water
and on the water a petrel
turned his head this way that way
didn't see me paddling.
Suddenly nothing but his tail
then nothing.
He plunged but not for me:
huge head upon the water
great hairy seal
giant head with giant eyes, mustache
all shining and dripping
and the seal came gently toward me.
Why didn't I harpoon him?
Was I sorry for him?
Was it the day, the spring day, the seal
playing in the sun
like me?

—*Anonymous*
(Eskimo Song
translated by Armand Schwerner)

173

Spring

Sound the flute!
Now it's mute.
Birds delight
Day and Night;
Nightingale
In the dale,
Lark in Sky,
Merrily,
Merrily, merrily, to welcome in the Year.

Little Boy,
Full of joy;
Little Girl,
Sweet and small;
Cock does crow,
So do you;
Merry voice,
Infant noise,
Merrily, merrily, to welcome in the Year.

Little Lamb
Here I am;
Come and lick
My white neck;

Let me pull
Your soft Wool;
Let me kiss
Your soft face;
Merrily, merrily, we welcome in the Year.

—*William Blake*

Spring Song

As my eyes search the prairie,
I feel the summer in the spring.

—*Anonymous*
(Chippewa Song
translated by Frances Densmore)

from *Corinna's Going a-Maying*

1

Get up, get up for shame, the blooming morn
Upon her wings presents the god unshorn.
    See how *Aurora* throws her fair
    Fresh-quilted colours through the air:

Get up, sweet slug-a-bed, and see
The dew-bespangled herb and tree.
Each flower has wept and bow'd towards the east
Above an hour since: yet you not dress'd;
Nay! not so much as out of bed?
When all the birds have matins said
And sung their thankful hymns, 'tis sin,
Nay, profanation to keep in,
Whenas a thousand virgins on this day
Spring, sooner than the lark, to fetch in May.

2

Rise and put on your foliage, and be seen
To come forth, like the spring-time, fresh and green,
And sweet as *Flora*. Take no care
For jewels for your gown or hair:
Fear not; the leaves will strew
Gems in abundance upon you:
Besides, the childhood of the day has kept,
Against you come, some *orient pearls* unwept;
Come and receive them while the light
Hangs on the dew-locks of the night:
And Titan on the eastern hill
Retires himself, or else stands still
Till you come forth. Wash, dress, be brief in
praying:
Few beads are best when once we go a-Maying.

Come, my *Corinna*, come; and, coming, mark
How each field turns a street, each street a park
  Made green and trimm'd with trees: see how
  Devotion gives each house a bough
  Or branch: each porch, each door ere this
  An ark, a tabernacle is,
Made up of white-thorn neatly interwove;
As if here were those cooler shades of love.
  Can such delights be in the street
  And open fields and we not see't?
  Come, we'll abroad; and let's obey
  The proclamation made for May:
And sin no more, as we have done, by staying;
But, my *Corinna*, come, let's go a-Maying.

There's not a budding boy or girl this day
But is got up, and gone to bring in May.
  A deal of youth, ere this, is come
  Back, and with *white-thorn* laden home.
  Some have despatch'd their cakes and cream
  Before that we have left to dream:
And some have wept, and woo'd, and plighted troth,
And chose their priest, ere we can cast off sloth:
  Many a green-gown has been given;
  Many a kiss, both odd and even:

Many a glance too has been sent
    From out the eye, love's firmament;
Many a jest told of the keys betraying
This night, and locks pick'd, yet we're not a-Maying.

4

Come, let us go while we are in our prime;
And take the harmless folly of the time.
    We shall grow old apace, and die
    Before we know our liberty.
    Our life is short, and our days run
    As fast away as does the sun;
And, as a vapour or a drop of rain,
Once lost, can ne'er be found again,
    So when or you or I are made
    A fable, song, or fleeting shade,
    All love, all liking, all delight
    Lies drowned with us in endless night.
Then while time serves, and we are but decaying,
Come, my *Corinna*, come, let's go a-Maying.

—Robert Herrick

Corinna's Not Going a-Maying

(The Lady addresses Mr. Herrick)

I like to sleep late on these fine spring mornings
Or lie in bed dreaming and half-awake.
And here's some fool babbling about Aurora
Under my window.   Oh for heaven's sake!

I don't intend to deck myself with flowers
And walk about spangled with gems of dew.
The other girls can play at being milkmaids.
I'd feel a perfect fool.   And wouldn't you?

But to your pastoral theme of sticky greenery
You bring in kisses as a counterpoint,
And talk of early morning assignations . . .
Aha!   I think we're coming to the point.

Life is so short! you cry.   But on this subject
Enough (enough, already) has been said.
Death's night is long, but last night isn't over.
Pack it in, Bob.   I'm going back to bed.

                              —*Gail White*

from *Pippa Passes*

The year's at the spring,
And day's at the morn;
    Morning's at seven;
The hill-side's dew-pearled;
The lark's on the wing;
The snail's on the thorn;
    God's in His heaven—
All's right with the world.
    —*Robert Browning*

Good Morning, Browning

God's in His heaven
Painting things blue;
I'm on the thorn,
The snail is too.
    —*Samuel Hoffenstein*

One More Reason to Celebrate

Hooray! Hooray!
The first of May;
Outdoor screwing
Begins today!
        —*Anonymous*

from *Rain in Summer*

How beautiful is the rain!
After the dust and heat,
In the broad and fiery street,
In the narrow lane,
How beautiful is the rain!

How it clatters along the roofs,
Like the tramp of hoofs!
How it gushes and struggles out
From the throat of the overflowing spout!
Across the window-pane
It pours and pours;
And swift and wide,

With a muddy tide,
Like a river down the gutter roars
The rain, the welcome rain!
—*Henry Wadsworth Longfellow*

A Description of the Morning

Now hardly here and there a hackney-coach
Appearing, showed the ruddy morn's approach.
Now Betty from her master's bed had flown,
And softly stole to discompose her own;
The slip-shod 'prentice from his master's door
Had pared the dirt and sprinkled round the floor.
Now Moll had whirled her mop with dext'rous airs,
Prepared to scrub the entry and the stairs.
The youth with broomy stumps began to trace
The kennel-edge, where wheels had worn the place.
The small-coal man was heard with cadence deep,
Till drowned in shriller notes of chimney-sweep:
Duns at his lordship's gate began to meet;
And brickdust Moll had screamed through half
     the street.
The turnkey now his flock returning sees,
Duly let out a-nights to steal for fees:

The watchful bailiffs take their silent stands,
And schoolboys lag with satchels in their hands.

—*Jonathan Swift*

You Are Young

(*Inscription in the autograph album of Rosa
Haggard, September 28, 1858*)

You are young, and I am older;
    You are hopeful, I am not—
Enjoy life, ere it grow colder—
    Pluck the roses ere they rot.

Teach your beau to heed the lay—
    That sunshine soon is lost in shade—
That *now's* as good as any day—
    To take thee, Rosa, ere she fade.

—*Abraham Lincoln*

Joy and Temperance

Joy and Temperance and Repose
Slam the door on the doctor's nose.

—*Anonymous*

A Toast

Here's to you and here's to me,
And here's to the girl with the well-shaped knee.
Here's to the man with his hand on her garter;
He hasn't got far yet, but he's a damn good starter.

—*Anonymous*

I Taste a Liquor Never Brewed

I taste a liquor never brewed—
From Tankards scooped in Pearl—
Not all the Vats upon the Rhine
Yield such an Alcohol!

Inebriate of Air—am I—
And Debauchee of Dew—

Reeling—thro endless summer days—
From inns of Molten Blue—

When "Landlords" turn the drunken Bee
Out of the Foxglove's door—
When Butterflies—renounce their "drams"—
I shall but drink the more!

Till Seraphs swing their snowy Hats—
And Saints—to windows run—
To see the little Tippler
Leaning against the—Sun—

    —Emily Dickinson

Anacreontic

Born I was to be old,
 And for to die here:
After that, in the mould
 Long for to lie here.
But before that day comes,
 Still I be bousing;
For I know, in the tombs
 There's no carousing.

    —Robert Herrick

from *Don Juan*

Man, being reasonable, must get drunk;
    The best of life is but intoxication:
Glory, the grape, love, gold, in these are sunk
    The hopes of all men, and of every nation;
Without their sap, how branchless were the trunk
    Of life's strange tree, so fruitful on occasion!
But to return—Get very drunk, and when
You wake with headache—you shall see what then!

        —*George Gordon, Lord Byron*

Rye Whiskey

I'll eat when I'm hungry,
    I'll drink when I'm dry;
If the hard times don't kill me,
    I'll lay down and die.

CHORUS

Rye whiskey, rye whiskey,
    Rye whiskey, I cry,
If you don't give me rye whiskey,
    I surely will die.

I'll tune up my fiddle,
   And I'll rosin my bow,
I'll make myself welcome,
   Wherever I go.

Beefsteak when I'm hungry,
   Red liquor when I'm dry,
Greenbacks when I'm hard up,
   And religion when I die.

They say I drink whiskey,
   My money's my own,
All them that don't like me,
   Can leave me alone.

               —Anonymous

King David and King Solomon

King David and King Solomon
   Led merry, merry lives,
With many, many lady friends
   And many, many wives;
But when old age crept over them,
   With many, many qualms,

King Solomon wrote the Proverbs
  And King David wrote the Psalms.
        —*James Ball Naylor*

Folly's Song

When wedding fiddles are a-playing,
        Huzza for folly O!
And when maidens go a-Maying,
        Huzza, etc.
When a milk-pail is upset,
        Huzza, etc.
And the clothes left in the wet,
        Huzza, etc.
When the barrel's set abroach,
        Huzza, etc.
When Kate Eyebrow keeps a coach,
        Huzza, etc.
When the pig is over-roasted,
        Huzza, etc.
And the cheese is over-toasted,
        Huzza, etc.

When Sir Snap is with his lawyer,
                 Huzza, etc.
And Miss Chip has kiss'd the sawyer;
                 Huzza, etc.

            —*John Keats*

A Little Lamb

Mary had a little lamb,
   She ate it with some mint sauce,
And everywhere that Mary went
   The lamb went too, of course.

            —*Anonymous*

The Menu

I beg you come to-night and dine.
A welcome waits you, and sound wine—
The Roederer chilly to a charm
As Juno's breath the claret warm,
The sherry of an ancient brand.
No Persian pomp, you understand—
A soup, a fish, two meats, and then

A salad fit for aldermen
(When aldermen, alas the days!
Were really worth their *mayonnaise*);
A dish of grapes whose clusters won
Their bronze in Carolinian sun;
Next, cheese—for you the Neufchâtel,
A bit of Cheshire likes me well;
Café au lait or coffee black,
With Kirsch or Kümmel or Cognac
(The German Band in Irving Place
By this time purple in the face);
Cigars and pipes.   These being through,
Friends shall drop in, a very few—
Shakespeare and Milton, and no more.
When these are guests I bolt the door,
With Not at Home to any one
Excepting Alfred Tennyson.

        —*Thomas Bailey Aldrich*

One-upmanship à la Carte

Seated al fresco at the Bistro Clementé,
The epicure said to the maitre, "I'm stuck!
Should I have your tasty linguine al dente,
Or would you suggest the maigret of duck?"

"Monsieur," said the maitre, unflappably dapper,
"Our special today is navarin of lamb;
But first you must try the carpaccio of snapper
Or else a terrine of split pea with ham."

The epicure snickered and studied the menu:
"Well, I see you have osso bucco today;
Or the paillard de veau might suit me, and then
    you
Could bring, for dessert, your famous soufflé."

But the maitre demurred, his gesture a no-no;
The epicure sighed, with a hint of dismay:
"Do you think I'd enjoy the lobster diablo
Or shrimp en cru with a dry Chardonnay?"

"Now look!" snapped the maitre. The lamb is
    what's tasty;
The duck and the veal are tougher than brass;
The seafood is frozen, the pasta is pasty—
And you, like the chef, are a pain in the ass!"

                    —*Ned Pastor*

Bacon and Greens

I have lived long enough to be rarely mistaken,
   And have my full share of Life's changeable
      scenes;
But my woes have been solaced by good Greens
      and Bacon,
   And my joys have been doubled by Bacon and
      Greens.

What a thrill of remembrance e'en now they
      awaken
   Of childhood's young morning and youth's merry
      scenes—
One day we had Greens and a plateful of Bacon,
   The next we had Bacon and a plateful of Greens.

          —*Anonymous*

On Being Asked How One Should Clean Mushrooms

A mushroom is a lovesome thing, God wot,
And porous too, so some good chefs will not
Allow a fresh one near the water spigot

For fear the thirsty fungal growth will swig it.
And once you let them start, there is no stopping
The swilling little buggers till they're sopping.
But others (I among them) say, "Oh bosh!
No mushroom suffers from a quickie wash."
And yes, a gentle brush can help to sweep
The sand from places where it tends to creep.
I call it "sand," though if you saw the muck
In which they grow, you surely would cry, "Yuck"
   And "Mercy, Maud" and "Oh my stars and
      garters,
If I fed that to my family, surely we would all
  of us, in the fullness of time, become martyrs."

               —*John J. Brugaletta*

The Cow's Revenge

Obligingly, the mild cow lets us quaff
The milk that she'd intended for her calf,
But takes revenge: In every pint she packs
A heavy cream to trigger heart attacks.

              —*X. J. Kennedy*

To Butter a Bagel

To butter a bagel
You need to finagle
Just to inveigle
The slithering spread
To the edge of the bread,
Avoiding the hole
Of this crisp Jewish roll
Lest globs of goo land
In the palm of your hand.

If you want to add extras
You'd better be dextrous
And nab the stray blocks
Of cream cheese and lox
That fall through the middle
Of this no-middle vittle.

     —*Alma Denny*

What a Friend
We Have in Cheeses!

or, Sing a Song of Liederkranz

Poets have been mysteriously silent on the subject of
cheese.

—*G. K. Chesterton*

What a friend we have in cheeses,
For no food more subtly pleases,
   Nor plays so vast a gastronomic part;
Cheese imported—not domestic—
For we all get indigestic
   From the pasteurizer's Kraft and sodden art.

No poem we shall ever see is
Quite as lovely as a Brie is,
   For the queen of cheese is what they call the
      Brie;
If you pay sufficient money
You will get one nice and runny,
   And you'll understand what foods these morsels
      be!

How we covet all the skills it
Takes in making Chevre or Tilsit,

But if getting basic Pot Cheese is your aim,
Take some simple curds and wheys, a
Bit of rennet—Lo! you've a Kaese!
    (Vich is what, in German, is a cheese's name.)

Good lasagna, its a-gotta
Mozzarella and Ricotta
    And a lotta freshly grated Parmesan;
With the latter *any* pasta
Will be eaten up much faster,
    For with Parmesan an added charm is on.

Ask your average padrone
What he thinks of Provolone,
    And the very word will set his eyes aflame;
Then go ask the bounteous Gina
Her reaction to Fontina—
    If you'll raise your eyes you'll see she feels the
        same.

A Pont-l'Evêque *au point!* What ho!
How our juices all will flow!
    But don't touch a Pont-l'Evêque beyond that
        stage,
For what you'll have, you'll surely find

Is just an overfragrant rind—
   There's no benefit to this *fromage* from age.

Claret, dear, not Coca-Cola,
When you're having Gorgonzola—
   Be particular to serve the proper wines;
Likewise pick a Beaune, not Coke for
Pointing up a Bleu or Roquefort—
   Bless the products of the bovines and the vines!

Ave Gouda! Ave Boursault!
Ave Oka even more so!
   Ave Neufchâtel! Saluto Port-Salut!
And another thing with cheeses—
Every allied prospect pleases—
   Ah cheese omelet! Ah Welsh rabbit! Ah fondue!

And we all know that "Say cheese" is
How a cameraman unfreezes
   A subject in a stiff, or shy, or dour way;
There's no other food so useful,
So bring on a whole cabooseful
   Of the stuff of life—the cheeses of the gourmet!
           —*William Cole*

Sonnet to a Stilton Cheese

Stilton, thou shouldst be living at this hour.
And so thou art. Nor losest grace thereby;
England has need of thee, and so have I—
She is a Fen. Far as the eye can scour,
League after grassy league from Lincoln tower
To Stilton in the fields, she is a Fen.
Yet this high cheese, by choice of fenland men,
Like a tall green volcano rose in power.

                —*G. K. Chesterton*

A Goose for the Sauce

Oh how greedy Mr. Cross is!
He's simply mad about rich sauces.
From overindulgence in a bordelaise
He's apt to end up drunk and disorderlaise,
But the sauce he awards a big A plus
Is made by a friend who drives a bus.
On vacation during the ragweed and pollen days
He enjoys a busman's hollandaise.

                —*Ogden Nash*

Picnic

Our Mama had a Goitre
Around which we'd reconnoitre
When the Weather grew too hot for Man or Beast.
We'd sit there in the Shade
Like Navvies newly-paid,
And Bangers! Bangers! Bangers was our Feast!

—*John Mella*

Trivial Observation

As every person knows,
   from Land's End up to Putney,
Earl Grey is a type of tea,
   whilst *Major* Grey's a chutney.

—*William Cole*

from *In Praise of Pie*

I'd like to weave a pretty rhyme
   To send my *Daily News.*
What shall I do?   In vain I woo

The too-exacting Muse;
In vain I coax the tyrant minx,
    And this the reason why:
She will not sing a plaguy thing,
    Because I've eaten pie.

A pretty pass it is, indeed,
    That I have reached at last,
If I, in spite of appetite,
    Must fast, and fast, and fast!
The one dear boon I am denied
    Is that for which I sigh.
Take all the rest that men hold best,
    But leave, oh, leave me pie!
                    —*Eugene Field*

Hours of Sleep

Nature requires five; custom gives seven;
Laziness takes nine, and wickedness eleven.
                    —*Anonymous*

Get Up, Get Up

Get up, get up, you lazy-head,
  Get up you lazy sinner,
We need those sheets for tablecloths,
  It's nearly time for dinner!
          —*Anonymous*

I Woke Up One Morning . . .

and i couldn't remember my name
or anything that had ever
happened to me

i thought it might be
amnesia

i went to see a doctor
he gave me a series of tests

he said the good news is
you do not have amnesia

the bad news is
you do not have a name and
nothing has ever happened to you

—*Dan Nielsen*

Reflection on the Fallibility of Nemesis

He who is ridden by a conscience
Worries about a lot of nonscience;
He without benefit of scruples
His fun and income soon quadruples.

—*Ogden Nash*

Party Knee

To drink in moderation, and to smoke
A minimal amount, and joke
Reservedly does not insure
Awaking from a party whole and pure.

Be we as temperate as the turtledove,
A soiree is an orgy of
This strange excess, unknown in France,
And Rome, and Nineveh: the upright stance.

When more than four forgather in our land,
We stand, and stand, and stand, and stand;
Thighs ache, and drowsy numbness locks
The bones between our pockets and our socks.

Forgive us, Prince of Easement, when from bed
With addled knees and lucid head
We leap at dawn, and sob, and beg
A buffered aspirin for a splitting leg.
                                    —*John Updike*

The Dance

In Breughel's great picture, The Kermess,
the dancers go round, they go round and
around, the squeal and the blare and the
tweedle of bagpipes, a bugle and fiddles
tipping their bellies (round as thick-
sided glasses whose wash they impound)

their hips and their bellies off balance
to turn them. Kicking and rolling about
the Fair Grounds, swinging their butts, those
shanks must be sound to bear up under such
rollicking measures, prance as they dance
in Breughel's great picture, The Kermess.

—*William Carlos Williams*

Obituary

Swank, who'd affect stretch limos to show off in,
Lies pleased as Punch here in a 12-foot coffin.

—*John Frederick Nims*

SEVEN

Around the World &
Back Again, or
matters geographical, historical,
political, & whatever else we can
throw in

205

Geography: A Song

There are no rocks
At Rockaway,
There are no sheep
At Sheepshead Bay,
There's nothing new
In Newfoundland,
And silent is
Long Island Sound.

—*Howard Moss*

To the Terrestrial Globe

by a Miserable Wretch

Roll on, thou ball, roll on!
Through pathless realms of Space
      Roll on!
What though I'm in a sorry case?
What though I cannot meet my bills?
What though I suffer toothache's ills?
What though I swallow countless pills?
  Never *you* mind!
      Roll on!

Roll on, thou ball, roll on!
Through seas of inky air
                    Roll on!
It's true I have no shirts to wear;
It's true my butcher's bill is due;
It's true my prospects all look blue—
But don't let that unsettle you:
    Never *you* mind!
                    Roll on!
                              [*It rolls on.*]
            —*W. S. Gilbert*

Sing a Song of Spillage

Sing a song of spillage—
    A tanker's fouled the shore;
Four-and-twenty black birds—
    They were white before.
        —*Frank Jacobs*

Cockles and Mussels

In Dublin's fair city,
Where the girls are so pretty,
   I first set my eyes on sweet Mollie Malone.
She wheeled her wheelbarrow
Through streets broad and narrow,
   Crying, "Cockles and mussels, alive, alive, oh!

CHORUS

   "Alive, alive, oh!
   Alive, alive, oh!"
   Crying, "Cockles and mussels, alive, alive, oh!"

She was a fishmonger,
But sure 'twas no wonder,
   For so were her father and mother before.
And they both wheeled their barrow
Through streets broad and narrow,
   Crying, "Cockles and mussels, alive, alive, oh!

She died of a fever,
And none could relieve her,
   And that was the end of sweet Mollie Malone.

But her ghost wheels her barrow
Through streets broad and narrow,
   Crying, "Cockles and mussels, alive, alive, oh!"

               —*Anonymous*

from *The City of Prague*

I dwelt in a city enchanted,
   And lonely, indeed, was my lot;
Two guineas a week, all I wanted,
   Was certainly all that I got.
Well, somehow I found it was plenty;
   Perhaps you may find it the same,
If—*if* you are just five-and-twenty,
   With industry, hope, and an aim:
Though the latitude's rather uncertain,
   And the longitude also is vague,
The persons I pity who know not the City,
   The beautiful city of Prague!

           —*William Jeffrey Prowse*

Cologne

In Köln, a town of monks and bones,
And pavements fanged with murderous stones,
And rags, and hags, and hideous wenches,
I counted two-and-seventy stenches,
All well defined, and separate stinks!
Ye nymphs that reign o'er sewers and sinks,
The river Rhine, it is well known,
Doth wash your city of Cologne;
But tell me, nymphs, what power divine
Shall henceforth wash the river Rhine?

—*Samuel Taylor Coleridge*

Hertfordshire Harmony

There was an old fellow of Tring,
Who, when somebody asked him to sing,
      Replied, "Ain't it odd?
      I can never tell *God*
Save the Weasel from *Pop Goes the King*."

—*Anonymous*

If Ever You Go to Dolgelly

If ever you go to Dolgelly
    Don't dine at the Lion Hotel;
For there's nothing to put in your belly
    And no one to answer the bell.
                —*Thomas Hughes*

British Weather

It is the merry month of May,
when everything is cold and grey,
the rain is dripping from the trees
and life is like a long disease,

the storm clouds hover round like ghouls,
the birds all sing, because they're fools,
and beds of optimistic flowers
are beaten down by thunder showers,

under a weak and watery sun
nothing seems to be much fun—
exciting as a piece of string,
this is the marvellous British Spring!
                —*Gavin Ewart*

The British Journalist

You cannot hope
or bribe or twist
(thank God!) the
British journalist.
But, seeing what
the man will do
unbribed, there's
no occasion to.

—*Humbert Wolfe*

from *H.M.S. Pinafore*

He is an Englishman!
    For he himself has said it,
    And it's greatly to his credit,
That he is an Englishman!
    For he might have been a Roosian,
    A French, or Turk, or Proosian,
Or perhaps Itali-an!
    But in spite of all temptations,
    To belong to other nations,

He remains an Englishman!
          Hurrah!
For the true-born Englishman!
          —*W. S. Gilbert*

Victorian

Miss with the vapours.
The claret and the oysters.
The curling papers.
Fat clergy in the cloisters.

Heavy squires hunting.
Pints of port and porter.
Grumbling and grunting.
Gothic bricks and mortar.

Fog in the dockyards.
Decorum at the Palace.
Blood in the stockyards.
Murder in the alleys.
          —*Gavin Ewart*

Homeward Bound

Day done, and homeward. Sardined agony,
   Arms clamped prisoners, spine in a question
      mark,
Each judders to the tin cacophony
   Of his pulsating Walkman. Finsbury Park*
Shovels fresh flesh into this human stew;
   Welded by sweat, stale beer and garlic fumes,
Closer than lovers in some loveless screw
   They sway mute unison as Hitchin* looms.
Stranger to stranger moulds, buttock to crotch,
   Sleek-groomed P.A. to tattooed skinhead oik; I'll
Swear British Rail has schemed this squalid botch
   To fit their view of Hell, like Bosch or Breughel.
Dante's *Inferno*, when compared to this,
Reads like a recipe for heavenly bliss.

                —D. A. Prince

*Commuter stations north of London

214

Lines

(*Composed after learning that the plan to raise a statue of him had been scotched.*)

England's ingratitude still blots
    The scutcheon of the brave and free;
I saved you from a million spots.
    And now you grudge a spot to me.
            —*Dr. Edward Jenner*

A Sleeper from the Amazon

A sleeper from the Amazon
Put nighties of his gra'mazon.
    The reason? That
    He was too fat
To get his own pajamas on.

            —*Anonymous*

215

Up the Orinoco

On an ancient paddle steamer,
   Aunt Louise and Uncle Bill
Travelled up the Orinoco, funds
   Supplied by grandpa's will.

Uncle Bill was keen on flora;
   Aunt Louise was ditto fish;
Both had felt the river journey
   Answered grandpa's dying wish.

How life differed on the river
   From that left behind in Wells:
Screeching birds and howling monkeys
   Took the place of tolling bells.

Sad to say, the ancient steamer
   Blew its boiler while en route,
With a roar that scared the natives
   And my poor dear aunt, to boot.

Blasted by the bursting boiler,
   Faster than a lightning flash,
Aunt L. arced across the water,
   Landing with a mighty splash.

Jungle creatures crouched in terror;
  Whirring wings obscured the sky;
Then a silence yet more frightening
  Followed poor Aunt's muffled cry.

Uncle Bill, vacation cancelled,
  Cursed his luck and, very cross,
Blamed my aunt for what had happened,
  Calling hers a "tiresome" loss.

Still, I bet the fierce piranha
Rated Aunt the top banana.
             —*Bruce E. Newling*

Some River Rhymes*

Down by the rancid River Rockaway
Sue got a wet foot, so she threw the sock away.
A trout cried, "Don't pollute, my pretty—
They drink this stuff in Jersey City."
             —*X. J. Kennedy*

Sailing one day on the Black Sea
Amazingly I saw a taxi.

217

That was strange but more spine-tinglish—
The taxi driver spoke good English.

—Edmund Conti

We punted on the Hellespont
And rowed around the Rhone.
But on the Inne we all fell out
And I Cam home alone.

—Gail White

When I was a young man
   on the Ganges banks,
I ran a small concession
   dispersing fries and franks;
One day a holy monk came up,
   head shaved and clad in yellow.
"Make Me One With Everything,"
   said this mystic fellow.

—William Cole

*verse form invented by William Cole

At the Dead Goat Saloon

It was the kind of night
when your pet goat
dies of toxic waste
on the shore of the Great Salt Lake
and your Osterizer
craps out on the first margarita;
no one you know or used to
has the same long-distance
service, and you get connected
with Point Barrow, Alaska—
a recorded message
from the Chamber of Commerce
boosting investment opportunities—
so you decide to invest
in a few long draughts
of dark, chewy Lowenbrau
and a good lamb curry
at the Dead Goat Saloon.

—David Lunde

Sir Edmund Hillary

Higgledy-piggledy
Sir Edmund Hillary
Climbed up Mount Everest
Just for the view.

Said to his Sherpa guides
Himalayatical,
"Now that one's up here, what
Does a chap do?"
—*Anthony Harrington*

Johann Gutenberg

Higgledy-piggledy
Publisher Gutenberg
Printing the Bible was
Sure he'd not fail

Knowing the Book had a
Cinemascopical
Nature ensuring a
Hollywood sale.
—*Anthony Harrington*

from *The Mikado*

To lay aloft in a howling breeze
    May tickle a landsman's taste,
But the happiest hour a sailor sees
    Is when he's down
    At an inland town,
With his Nancy on his knees, yeo ho!
    And his arm around her waist!
        —*W. S. Gilbert*

On Cabbages and Kings

The cabbages lie *tête-à-tête*
Like Louis and his Antoinette,
Reminders of the awful fate
That sometimes falls to heads of state.
        —*Bob McKenty*

Impromptu on Charles II

God bless our good and gracious King,
  Whose promise none relies on;
Who never said a foolish thing,
  Nor ever did a wise one.
    —*John Wilmot, Earl of Rochester*

Henry VIII

When he decreed
  He'd be rewedded,
They had to heed
  Or be beheaded.

He lost his head
  To Anne Boleyn,
He his who said
  It was a sin.

"No more, no more!"
  Sir Thomas cried,
"No more of More!"
  The king replied.

222

It's sad, but if More *had*
Had more success,
We never would have had
Queen Bess.
—*Henry G. Fischer*

The Classes

The lower classes,
With vivid lashes,
Fix oily and redolent fricassees and hashes.

The middle classes,
Whose goal is stasis,
Practice with their sons lateral or forward passes.

The upper classes,
Like certain rare elements are almost massless,
And lounge and count their money like sheiks or
　　rajahs or czars or pashas.
—*John Mella*

The Poverty Programs

Are planned to make things better and not worse.
But by the time the billions get passed down
Someone's absconded with the integers
And let the zeroes help the poor alone.
—Howard Nemerov

A Fair Division

Another Irish landlord gone to grass,
Slain by the bullets of the tenant class!
Pray, good agrarians, what wrong requires
Such foul redress? Between you and the squires
All Ireland's parted with an even hand—
For you have all the ire, they all the land.
—Ambrose Bierce

from *The Pirates of Penzance*

When a felon's not engaged in his employment,
  Or maturing his felonious little plans,
His capacity for innocent enjoyment
  Is just as great as any other man's.
Our feelings we with difficulty smother
  When constabulary duty's to be done:
Ah, take one consideration with another,
  A policeman's lot is not a happy one.

When the enterprising burglar's not a-burgling,
  And the cut-throat isn't occupied in crime,
He loves to hear the little brook a-gurgling,
  And listen to the merry village chime.
When the coster's finished jumping on his mother,
  He loves to lie a-basking in the sun:
Ah, take one consideration with another,
  A policeman's lot is not a happy one!
                                    —*W. S. Gilbert*

The Unknown Citizen

*(To JS/07/M/378 This Marble Monument
Is Erected by the State)*

He was found by the Bureau of Statistics to be
One against whom there was no official
    complaint,
And all the reports on his conduct agree
That, in the modern sense of an old-fashioned
    word, he was a saint,
For in everything he did he served the Greater
    Community.
Except for the War till the day he retired
He worked in a factory and never got fired,
But satisfied his employers, Fudge Motors Inc.
Yet he wasn't a scab or odd in his views,
For his Union reports that he paid his dues
(Our report on his Union shows it was sound),
And our Social Psychology workers found
That he was popular with his mates and liked a
    drink.
The Press are convinced that he bought a paper
    every day
And that his reactions to advertisements were
    normal in every way.

Policies taken out in his name prove that he was
    fully insured,
And his Health-card shows he was once in
    hospital but left it cured.
Both Producers Research and High-Grade Living
    declare
He was fully sensible to the advantages of the
    Installment Plan
And had everything necessary to the Modern Man,
A phonograph, a radio, a car and a frigidaire.
Our researchers into Public Opinion are content
That he held the proper opinions for the time of
    year;
When there was peace, he was for peace; when
    there was war, he went.
He was married and added five children to the
    population,
Which our Eugenist says was the right number for
    a parent of his generation,
And our teachers report that he never interfered
    with their education.
Was he free? Was he happy? The question is
    absurd:
Had anything been wrong, we should certainly
    have heard.

                                    —*W. H. Auden*

My First Try for Votes

Uneasy in my first campaign,
  I feared the likely ridicule,
but got up nerve and neared
  some loafers I saw shooting pool.

I caught the eye of an older man
  who seemed to know who I might be.
When I walked up to him to speak,
  he cocked a bleary eye at me.

"Now wait, don't tell me who you are,"
  he shouted out. I stood in dread.
Bystanders paused. I blabbed my name.
  He frowned. "Naw, that ain't it," he said.

—*Jimmy Carter*

On a Deceased Office-Seeker

An Epitaph

At last elected this low place to fill,
No longer running now, but lying still.

—*Laurence Perrine*

On Louisiana Politics

The politician, like the tabby's young,
attempts to wash his backside with his tongue.
                                    —*Gail White*

from *To a Noisy Politician*

On coaches, now, gay coats of arms are wore
By *some,* who hardly had a coat before:
Silk gowns instead of homespun, now, are seen,
And, sir, 'tis true ('twixt me and you)
That some have grown prodigious fat,
That were prodigious lean!
                                    —*Philip Freneau*

Politician in the Pew

His very public piety
Achieved such notoriety
That, just as he'd suspected,
In time he was elected.

229

Accomplishing his purpose thus,
He grew less sanctimonious
Until, a private citizen
Once more, he breathed his last "Amen,"
And—never went to church again.

—*Maureen Cannon*

Inaugural Message

A President may never win
   The hearts of all our fickle rout.
One happy day we swear him in,
   But after that we cuss him out.

—*Arthur Guiterman*

EIGHT

Literary Hijinks
&
Parodies

from *Poeta Fit, Non Nascitur*

"How shall I be a poet?
  How shall I write in rhyme:
You told me once 'the very wish
  Partook of the sublime.'
Then tell me how! Don't put me off
  With your 'another time!'"

The old man smiled to see him,
  To hear his sudden sally;
He liked the lad to speak his mind
  Enthusiastically;
And thought "There's no hum-drum in him,
  Nor any shilly-shally."

"And would you be a poet
  Before you've been to school?
Ah, well! I hardly thought you
  So absolute a fool.
First learn to be spasmodic—
  A very simple rule.

"For first you write a sentence,
  And then you chop it small;

Then mix the bits, and sort them out
   Just as they chance to fall:
The order of the phrases makes
   No difference at all.

"Then, if you'd be impressive,
   Remember what I say,
That abstract qualities begin
   With capitals alway:
The True, the Good, the Beautiful—
   Those are the things that pay!"
            —*Lewis Carroll*

Child Labor in Literary Sweatshops

I

Among the literary mills
   Where story-books are made,
I saw a sad, anemic lad
   A-plying of his trade.
The novel he was working on
   Had such a heavy plot

If it had spilled, it might have killed
    That willing little tot.

II

"O child!" I cried, "this is no place
    For one so very young—
Take care, beware! this close, stale air
    May hurt each little lung.
O lay aside your pen and ink"—
    The Infant shook his head;
"Ah, would I might—but I must write
    To earn our daily bread.

III

"My father, ere he took to drink,
    Had literary skill,
But since his fall we children all
    Were prenticed to the mill.
My brother Ben (he's almost ten)
    Turns out the novelettes
And sister Kate (she's only eight)
    Works over storiettes.

IV

"But, being younger than the rest,
    They work me like a dog
A-tying knots in half-baked plots
    And building dialogue.

234

And sometimes when the trade is rushed
    I labor overtime
At outdoor scenes for magazines
    And seasonable rhyme.

                        v

"O, sir, to cavil or complain
    We're really very loath;
Although this here dense atmosphere
    Must surely stunt our growth—
Perhaps them folks what read our books
    Can guess our fate so crool;
We want to be like others, free.
    We want to go to school!"

                        vi

I left the literary mill
    In gloomy mood indeed—
It makes me wild to think some child
    Has written what I read.
Child-labor must be crushed! Reform
    Must trace the matter home!
(I'll send these views to Mr. Hughes
    And William T. Jerome.)

                        —*Wallace Irwin*

To an Undiscerning Critic

Sure, there are times when one cries with acidity,
"Where are the limits of human stupidity?"
Here is a critic who says as a platitude,
That I am guilty because "'in ingratitude,
Sherlock, the sleuth hound, with motives ulterior,
Sneers at Poe's Dupin as very 'inferior.'"

Have you not learned, my esteemed commentator,
That the created is not the creator?
As the creator I've praised to satiety
Poe's Monsieur Dupin, his skill and variety,
And have admitted that in my detective work,
I owe to my model a deal of selective work.
                    —*Arthur Conan Doyle*

The Poet's Fate

What is a modern Poet's fate?
To write his thought upon a slate;
The Critic spits on what is done,
Gives it a wipe—and all is gone.
                    —*Thomas Hood*

To Christopher North

You did late review my lays,
   Crusty Christopher;
You did mingle blame and praise,
   Rusty Christopher.
When I learnt from whom it came,
I forgave you all the blame,
   Musty Christopher;
I could *not* forgive the praise,
   Fusty Christopher.

           —*Alfred, Lord Tennyson*

To My Least Favorite Reviewer

When I was young, just starting at our game,
I ambitioned to be christlike, and forgive thee.
For a mortal Jew that proved too proud an aim;
Now it's my humbler hope just to outlive thee.

        —*Howard Nemerov*

Grinding Teeth

Nothing in the life of Lord Byron
Pleases me so much as the fact that his dentist
Said he was damaging his teeth
By grinding them in his sleep,
And I think how many Literary Critics
Are probably doing the same thing
This very night.

—*Christopher Morley*

Experimental

Fadd publishes his "experiments," verse and prose.
Like a doctor showing his corpses, you suppose?

—*John Frederick Nims*

Yet Another Anthology of
New American Poets

Alike as peas they look, these bards quick-frozen.
How many are so called, how many chosen.

—*X. J. Kennedy*

Two Men Wrote a Lexicon

Two men wrote a lexicon, Liddell and Scott;
Some parts were clever but some parts were not.
Hear, all ye learned, and read me this riddle:
Which part wrote Scott, and which part wrote
    Liddell?

—*Anonymous*

As I Was Laying on the Green

As I was laying on the green,
A small English book I seen.
Carlyle's *Essay on Burns* was the edition,
So I left it laying in the same position.

—*Anonymous*

Patience

A *Paraphrase on Job* we see
    By Young: it loads the shelf:
He who can read one-half must be
    Patient as Job himself.

           —*W. S. Landor*

A Modern Poet

Crossing at rush hour the Walt Whitman Bridge,
He stopped at the Walt Whitman Shopping
    Center
And bought a paperback copy of *Leaves of Grass*.
Fame *is* the spur, he figured; given a Ford
Foundation Fellowship, he'd buy a Ford.

           —*Howard Nemerov*

A Rhymester

Jem writes his verses with more speed
    Than the printer's boy can set 'em;

Quite as fast as we can read,
  And only not so fast as we forget 'em.
                    —*Samuel Taylor Coleridge*

What Hundred Books

"What hundred books are best, think you?" I said,
  Addressing one devoted to the pen.
He thought a moment, then he raised his head:
  "I hardly know—I've only written ten."
                    —*John Kendrick Bangs*

On Scott's
"The Field of Waterloo"

On Waterloo's ensanguined plain
Lie tens of thousands of the slain;
But none, by sabre or by shot,
Fell half so flat as Walter Scott.
                    —*Thomas, Lord Erskine*

On Oliver Goldsmith

An Epitaph

Here lies Nolly Goldsmith,
    for shortness called Noll,
Who wrote like an angel,
    but talked like poor Poll.
       —*David Garrick*

The Fool and the Poet

Sir, I admit your general rule,
That every poet is a fool,
But you yourself may serve to show it,
That every fool is not a poet.
       —*Alexander Pope*

Alley Cat Serenade

Come into the garden, Fred,
For the neighborhood Tabby is gone.
Come into the garden, Fred.
I have nothing but my flea collar on,
And the scent of catnip has gone to my head.
I'll wait by the screen-door till dawn.

The fireflies court in the sweet-gum tree.
The nightjar calls from the pine,
And she seems to say in her rhapsody,
"Oh, mustard-brown Fred be mine!"
The full moon lights my whiskers afire,
And the fur goes erect on my spine.

I hear the frogs in the muddy lake
Croaking from shore to shore.
They've one swift summer to soothe their ache.
In autumn they sing no more.
So ignore me now, and you'll hear my meow
As I scratch all night at the door.

—*Dana Gioia*

Miss Dickinson
Goes to the Office

Because I could not stop for lunch,
    it kindly stopped for me.
The lunch tray held a lemon sponge
    and watercress and tea.

I heard a fly buzz—in the Slaw—
    immortal for an hour.
The tea was hot—a small Brazil—
    although the cream was sour.

Since then 'tis centuries, yet each
    seems shorter than the day
I first surmised the weekend was
    five working days away.
        —*Gail White*

Jacob

He dwelt among "Apartments let,"
    About five stories high;
A man, I thought, that none would get,
    And very few would try.

A boulder, by a larger stone
    Half hidden in the mud,
Fair as a man when only one
    Is in the neighborhood.

He lived unknown, and few could tell
    When Jacob was not free;
But he has got a wife—and O!
    The difference to me!
                —*Phoebe Cary*

"What a Booboo," said Oedipus Rex

"What a booboo," said Oedipus Rex.
"Here, I've called down this horrible hex.
        I've wed Mother—how rough!—
        And trashed Dad—it's enough
To turn anyone sour on sex."
                —*X. J. Kennedy*

Chaucerian Sonnet:
A Tale of the Clark of Kent

A Clark there was of Kent also
That unto comic strips longe ygo
Made a byggen splash, tho lene was his readers'
    brains
As if they didn't knowen to come out of rain.
This Clark was a reporter, mild and just,
Who for Lois Lane hungered with great lust,
But this meek carl—and this is God's own truth—
Could change himself in any payphone booth
Into a hero faster than a speeding duck
(Some folkes haven all the luck!)
& flew villains toward Lawe's iron reche
For gladly would he lerne and gladly teche
That Crime payeth not & is not too sound
When Superman leapeth over buildings with a
    single bound.

                    —*Louis Phillips*

Salty Bore

It was an ancient mariner,
And he stoppeth one of three;
The two unstoppeth carrieth on—
The stoppeth cried, "Why me?"

—*William Cole*

Haiku

O.K., all you frogs—
Everyone out of the pond
And form three lines.

—*Edmund Conti*

The Balls

*(A basketball warmup as reported
by Edgar Allan Poe)*

Hear the chatter of the balls—
Basketballs!

Hear the echoes of their prattle rattle, rattle off
the walls.
Hear them stutter, stutter, stutter
On the floorboards of the gym.
Hear the grumbles that they utter
And the mumbles that they mutter
To the backboard and the rim
And the gibberish
Of their swish, swish, swish,
In the discombobulation that cacophonously calls
From the balls, balls, balls, balls
Balls, balls, balls—
The empty-headed babble of the balls.

—*Bob McKenty*

Those Annual Bills

*(A parody on "Those Evening Bells"
by Thomas Moore)*

The annual bills! these annual bills!
How many a song their discord trills
Of "truck" consumed, enjoyed, forgot,
Since I was skinned by last year's lot!

Those joyous beans are passed away;
Those onions blithe, O where are they?
Once loved, lost, mourned—*now* vexing ILLS
Your shades troop back in annual bills!

And so 'twill be when I'm aground—
These yearly duns will still go round,
While other bards, with frantic quills,
Shall damn and *damn* these annual bills!
                                        —*Mark Twain*

The Duke's Version of Hamlet's Soliloquy in Huckleberry Finn

To be or not to be; that is the bare bodkin
That makes calamity of so long life;
For who would fardels bear, till Birnam Wood do
        come to Dunsinane,
But that the fear of something after death
Murders the innocent sleep,
Great nature's second course,
And makes us rather sling the arrows of
        outrageous fortune
Than fly to others that we know not of.

There's the respect must give us pause:
Wake Duncan with thy knocking! I would thou
    couldst;
For who would bear the whips and scorns of time,
The oppressor's wrong, the proud man's
    contumely,
The law's delay, and the quietus which his pangs
    might take,
In the dead waste and middle of the night, when
    churchyards yawn
In customary suits of solemn black,
But that the undiscovered country from whose
    bourne no traveler returns,
Breathes forth contagion on the world,
And thus the native hue of resolution, like the
    poor cat i' the adage,
Is sicklied o'er with care,
And all the clouds that lowered o'er our
    housetops,
With this regard their currents turn awry,
And lose the name of action.
'Tis a consummation devoutly to be wished. But
    soft you, the fair Ophelia:
Ope not thy ponderous and marble jaws,
But get thee to a nunnery—go!
                —*Mark Twain*

from Variations of an Air: Composed on Having to Appear in a Pageant as Old King Cole

If Walt Whitman Had Written Old King Cole

Me clairvoyant,
Me conscious of you, old camarado,
Needing no telescope, lorgnette, field-glass,
      opera-glass, myopic pince-nez,
Me piercing two thousand years with eye naked
      and not ashamed;
The crown cannot hide you from me;
Musty old feudal-heraldic trappings cannot hide
      you from me,
I perceive that you drink.
(I am drinking with you. I am as drunk as you are.)
I see you are inhaling tobacco, puffing, smoking,
      spitting
(I do not object to your spitting),
You prophetic of American largeness,
You anticipating the broad masculine manners of
      these States;

I see in you also there are movements, tremors,
        tears, desire for the melodious,
I salute your three violinists, endlessly making
        vibrations,
Rigid, relentless, capable of going on for ever;
They play my accompaniment; but I shall take no
        notice of any accompaniment;
I myself am a complete orchestra.
So long.

— *G. K. Chesterton*

Thoughts on Rereading
"Don Juan"

The reprobate pursues the virtuous woman
    With purposes extremely reprehensible;
He swoops upon his prey as with a Grumman
    Jet plane. To this she cannot be insensible.
I loathe the reprobate; there is no room in
    My mind to make defense of th' indefensible.
Yet surely any scientist of stature'll
Admit the reprobate's behavior's natural.

Then fie on Nature, which approves begetters
    Of by-blows! Let us rather give our plaudit
To blameless men adjusting carburetors,
    To auditors in agony of audit,
To red-eyed commentators on belles-letters,
    To the bank's guards 'gainst crooks who would
        defraud it,
To those who cheat the grinning doom pursuing
    'em
By pressing pants, and advertising chewing gum.
                    —*Morris Bishop*

Us Potes

Swift was sweet on Stella;
    Poe had his Lenore;
Burns' fancy turned to Nancy
    And a dozen more.

Pope was quite a trifler;
    Goldsmith was a case;
Byron'd flirt with any skirt
    From Liverpool to Thrace.

Sheridan philandered;
   Shelley, Keats, and Moore
All were there with some affair
   Far from lit'rachoor.

Fickle is the heart of
   Each immortal bard.
Mine alone is made of stone—
   Gotta work too hard.
          —*Franklin P. Adams*

Clothes

In Shakespeare's plays
Nobody knows
For days and days,
Till the very end,
His closest friend
If he's changed his clothes.

Prospero has
But to put on his hat
And he's what he was,
A duke, like that!

They gladly aver,
Who knew him before,
"You are what you were
When you wear what you wore."
—*Henry G. Fischer*

Fear Itself

FDR said it foremost
having used as his ghost

writer Emerson, Emerson
(also Thoreau & the Duke of Wellington)

having brought home his Bacon, Bacon
having reaped Montaigne, Montaigne

having absorbed Publilius Cyrus, Publilius
when timorous

(of death in particular)
having plucked it from the vernacular

for, as immortal Seneca has said
(with all the generous dead)

The best ideas are common property.
He also said, What fools these mortals be.
Copyright nineteen eight-one, Bonnie
    Jacobson

Optometrist and Poet

"Your far vision's good," said the doctor.
"Hills, trees, birds—you can see them all.
But your near vision's shot to hell.
You need half glasses to correct the blur."

*"Doctor, doctor, would that you could heal
My life as simply as you fix my eyes.
Although I'll try your glasses on for size,
Things close to me are always shot to hell."*

—*Dick Allen*

Defending the Canon

The stooping scholars labor, hot
  To keep intact the status quo
By proving Hawthorne Hottentot
  And Milton's mom a Navajo.

—X. J. Kennedy

A Comparative Study
Into the Major Factors
Contributing to a
Recognizable Differentiation
Between Prose and Poetry

Whereas the prose
more explicitly flows,

the verse
is terse.

—Marsh Cassady

Vanity Plates

To help promote his magazine,
to help increase its fame,
an editor ordered license plates
with the magazine's name.

Now, when he parks illegally,
he deals with police ambitions;
instead of tickets under the wipers
he gets story submissions!
— *Lawrence Schimel*

Found in Poets' Market '94

No curse words in poems,
little or no name-dropping,
no naming of consumer products,
no two page poems, no humor,
no bias writing . . .
9–30 lines, poems with hope.
— *Marjorie Power*

On Receiving a Contract to Translate The Iliad

Wise up, my boy! Give up the hell
of writing books you'll never sell,
and learn to take naughty delight
in selling books you'll never write.
　　　　　—Richard Moore

Directions for Remodeling Old Verse

A comma or so,
And a sinister row
Of periods there in the middle,
Might make it appear
Rather subtle and queer,
And give it the air of a riddle.

Italics are nice,
So I'll throw in a slice,
And leave off the capital letter,

With a dash for suspense—
If it doesn't make sense,
At least it may *look* a lot better.
    —*Margaret Fishback*

NINE

Portraits in All Shapes & Sizes,
many in epigram, limerick, & clerihew forms

To Mistress Margaret Hussey

Merry Margaret,
As midsummer flower,
Gentle as falcon
Or hawk of the tower:
With solace and gladness,
Much mirth and no madness,
All good and no badness;
So joyously,
So maidenly,
So womanly
Her demeaning
In every thing,
Far, far passing
That I can indite,
Or suffice to write
Of Merry Margaret
As midsummer flower,
Gentle as falcon
Or hawk of the tower.
As patient and still
And as full of good will
As fair Isaphill,
Coriander,

Sweet pomander,
Good Cassander,
Steadfast of thought,
Well made, well wrought,
Far may be sought
Ere that ye can find
So courteous, so kind
    As Merry Margaret,
    This midsummer flower,
Gentle as falcon
Or hawk of the tower.
        —John Skelton

On a Female Rope-Dancer

Whilst in her prime and bloom of years,
    Fair Celia trips the rope,
Alternately she moves our fears,
    Alternately our hope.

But when she sinks, or rises higher,
    Or graceful does advance,
We know not which we most admire,
    The dancer, or the dance.
        —Anonymous

Aunt Helen

Miss Helen Slingsby was my maiden aunt,
And lived in a small house near a fashionable
    square
Cared for by servants to the number of four.
Now when she died there was silence in heaven
And silence at her end of the street.
The shutters were drawn and the undertaker
    wiped his feet—
He was aware that this sort of thing had occurred
    before.
The dogs were handsomely provided for,
But shortly afterwards the parrot died too.
The Dresden clock continued ticking on the
    mantelpiece,
And the footman sat upon the dining-table
Holding the second housemaid on his knees—
Who had always been so careful while her
    mistress lived.

—T. S. Eliot

Father William

"You are old, Father William," the young man said,
  "And your hair has become very white;
And yet you incessantly stand on your head—
  Do you think, at your age, it is right?"

"In my youth," Father William replied to his son,
  "I feared it might injure the brain;
But, now that I'm perfectly sure I have none,
  Why, I do it again and again."

"You are old," said the youth, "as I mentioned
    before,
  And have grown most uncommonly fat;
Yet you turned a back-somersault in at the door—
  Pray, what is the reason of that?"

"In my youth," said the sage, as he shook his gray
    locks,
  "I kept all my limbs very supple
By the use of this ointment—one shilling the box—
  Allow me to sell you a couple?"

"You are old," said the youth, "and your jaws are
      too weak
  For anything tougher than suet;
Yet you finished the goose, with the bones and the
      beak—
  Pray, how did you manage to do it?"

"In my youth," said his father, "I took to the law,
  And argued each case with my wife;
And the muscular strength, which it gave to my
      jaw,
  Has lasted the rest of my life."

"You are old," said the youth, "one would hardly
      suppose
  That your eye was as steady as ever;
Yet you balanced an eel on the end of your nose—
  What made you so awfully clever?"

"I have answered three questions, and that is
      enough,"
  Said his father, "don't give yourself airs!
Do you think I can listen all day to such stuff?
  Be off, or I'll kick you down stairs!"

                    —*Lewis Carroll*

Father William

"You are old, Father William," the young man said,
  "And your hair now should be very white;
But it's black and it's bushy all over your head;
  Do you think, at your age, this is right?"

"It's touched up," Father William replied to his son,
  "And with transplants my baldness is ended;
Though I'm now 84, I appear 41,
  And the chicks think I'm groovy and splendid."

"You are old," said the youth, "and I thought I
    would find
  That your face would be sagging and wrinkling;
But your skin is as smooth as a baby's behind
  And of lines there is scarcely an inkling."

"Had a face-lift," the old man replied, "just last
    year;
  Cost a bundle, but now I feel human;
I used to come on like Redd Foxx or Will Geer,
  But now I'm hot stuff like Paul Newman."

"You are old," said the youth, "for despite your
    new look,

You are bogged down in hopeless senility;
With chicks you come off as a helpless old
    schnook,
    Despite all your claims of virility."

"Shut your face," Father William replied; "though
    it's true
    That I purchased new glands last September,
Whatever I'd hoped for my body to do,
    My mind is too old to remember."
                —*Frank Jacobs*

On Queen Caroline

    Most Gracious Queen, we thee implore
    To go away and sin no more,
    But if that effort be too great,
    To go away at any rate.
                —*Anonymous*

Lord Finchley

Lord Finchley tried to mend the Electric Light
Himself.   It struck him dead: and serve him right!
It is the business of the wealthy man
To give employment to the artisan.

—Hilaire Belloc

Lord Heygate

Lord Heygate had a troubled face,
His furniture was commonplace—
The sort of Peer who well might pass
For someone of the middle class.
I do not think you want to hear
About this unimportant Peer.

—Hilaire Belloc

On the
Hon. George Nathaniel Curzon,
Commoner of Balliol

My name is George Nathaniel Curzon,
I am a most superior person.
My cheeks are pink, my hair is sleek,
I dine at Blenheim twice a week.

—*J. W. Mackail & Cecil Spring-Rice*

Sir Arthur Balfour,
First Lord of the Admiralty,
Goes Out for a Game of Golf

I was playing golf that day
   When the Germans landed,
All our soldiers ran away,
   All our ships were stranded.
Such were my surprise and shame
They almost put me off my game.

—*Anonymous*

Epigram on Sir Roger Phillimore (1810–1885) and His Brother, George Phillimore

When Nature dreamt of making bores,
She formed a brace of Phillimores;
Sooner than make a Phillimost,
Nature herself would yield the ghost.

—*Anonymous*

from *The Masque of Balliol*

First come I. My name is JOWETT.
There's no knowlege but I know it.
I am Master of this College,
What I don't know isn't knowledge.

—*Henry Charles Beeching*

On the Painter Val Prinsep

There is a creator called God,
Whose creations are some of them odd.
    I maintain, and I shall,
    The creation of Val
Reflects little credit on God.

—*Dante Gabriel Rossetti*

To a Blockhead

You beat your pate, and fancy wit will come:
Knock as you please, there's nobody at home.

—*Alexander Pope*

To Doctor Empiric

When men a dangerous disease did 'scape
Of old, they gave a cock to Esculape:
Let me give two, that doubly am got free—
From my disease's danger, and from thee.

—*Ben Jonson*

On Sir John Hill, M.D., Playwright

For physic and farces his equal there scarce is;
His farces are physic; his physic a farce is.
—*David Garrick*

I Do Not Love Thee, Doctor Fell

I do not love thee, Doctor Fell,
The reason why I cannot tell;
But this alone I know full well,
I do not love thee, Doctor Fell.
—*Thomas Brown*

A Financier

His wishes state, "When I rescind my life,
Lay me beside my one and only wife."
His lawyer reads and, as instructed, locks
His ashes in his safe-deposit box.
—*X. J. Kennedy*

The Old Radical

The burning cause that lit his days
 When he was younger came to harm.
Now Hate's impoverished charcoal blaze
 Is all that keeps him warm.
 —*Phyllis McGinley*

On a Curate's
Complaint of Hard Duty

I march'd three miles through scorching sand,
With zeal in heart, and notes in hand;
I rode four more to Great St. Mary,
Using four legs, when two were weary:
To three fair virgins I did tie men,
In the close bands of pleasing Hymen;
I dipp'd two babes in holy water,
And purified their mother after.
Within an hour and eke a half,
I preach'd three congregations deaf;
Where, thundering out, with lungs long-winded,
I chopp'd so fast, that few there minded.
My emblem, the laborious sun,

Saw all these mighty labours done
Before one race of his was run.
All this perform'd by Robert Hewit:
What mortal else could e'er go through it!
—*Jonathan Swift*

from *The Pirates of Penzance*

I am the very model of a modern Major-General,
I've information vegetable, animal, and mineral;
I know the kings of England, and I quote the
    fights historical,
From Marathon to Waterloo, in order categorical;
I'm very well acquainted, too, with matters
    mathematical,
I understand equations, both the simple and
    quadratical;
About binomial theorem I'm teeming with a lot
    o' news,
With interesting facts about the square of the
    hypotenuse.
I'm very good at integral and differential calculus,
I know the scientific names of beings animalculous.

In short, in matters vegetable, animal, and mineral,
I am the very model of a modern Major-General.

I know our mythic history—King Arthur's and
    Sir Caradoc's,
I answer hard acrostics, I've a pretty taste for
    paradox;
I quote in elegiacs all the crimes of Heliogabalus,
In conics I can floor peculiarities parabolous.
I tell undoubted Raphaels from Gerard Dows
    and Zoffanies,
I know the croaking chorus from the "Frogs" of
    Aristophanes;
Then I can hum a fugue, of which I've heard the
    music's din afore,
And whistle all the airs from that confounded
    nonsense "Pinafore."
Then I can write a washing-bill in Babylonic
    cuneiform,
And tell you every detail of Caractacus's uniform.
In short, in matters vegetable, animal, and mineral,
I am the very model of a modern Major-General.

In fact, when I know what is meant by "mamelon"
    and "ravelin,"
When I can tell at sight a Chassepôt rifle from a
    javelin,

When such affairs as *sorties* and surprises I'm
      more wary at,
And when I know precisely what is meant by
      Commissariat,
When I have learnt what progress has been made
      in modern gunnery,
When I know more of tactics than a novice in a
      nunnery,
In short, when I've a smattering of elementary
      strategy,
You'll say a better Major-Gener*al* has never *sat* a
      gee—
For my military knowledge, though I'm plucky and
      adventury,
Has only been brought down to the beginning of
      the century.
But still in learning vegetable, animal, and
      mineral,
I am the very model of a modern Major-General!
           —*W. S. Gilbert*

Solomon Grundy

Solomon Grundy,
Born on a Monday,
Christened on Tuesday,
Married on Wednesday,
Took ill on Thursday,
Worse on Friday,
Died on Saturday,
Buried on Sunday,
This is the end
Of Solomon Grundy.

—*Anonymous*

For a Lady I Know

She even thinks that up in heaven
    Her class lies late and snores,
While poor black cherubs rise at seven
    To do celestial chores.

—*Countee Cullen*

What Kind of Guy Was He?

Just so you shouldn't have to ask again,
He was the kind of guy that if he said
Something and you were the kind of guy that said
You can say that again, he'd say it again.

—*Howard Nemerov*

For a Pessimist

He wore his coffin for a hat,
    Calamity his cape,
While on his face a death's-head sat
    And waved a bit of crape.

—*Countee Cullen*

Two Versions: After a Famous French Poet

Quatrain

Je suis Françoys dont il me poise,
Ne de Paris empres Pontoise
Et de la corde d'une toise
Scaura mon col que mon cul poise.
—*François Villon*

Villon's Quatrain

I am François, to my great dismay,
Born in Paris, up Pontoise way;
By a fathom of hempen cord I'll sway
While my neck discovers what my buttocks weigh.
—*David Lunde*

280

L'Enfant Glacé

When Baby's cries grew hard to bear
I popped him in the Frigidaire.
I never would have done so if
I'd known that he'd be frozen stiff.
My wife said: "George, I'm so unhappé!
Our darling's now completely *frappé*."

—*Harry Graham*

Opportunity

When Mrs. Gorm (Aunt Eloise)
Was stung to death by savage bees,
Her husband (Prebendary Gorm)
Put on his veil, and took the swarm.
He's publishing a book next May
On "How to Make Bee-keeping Pay."

—*Harry Graham*

"Look Away"

From Richmond, she was, or Norfolk—
Never sick a day in her life, nor well, either:
just strong enough to run everybody
and everything, just weak enough
never to raise her voice.
                          Anyhow,
she died most unexpectedly in her sleep.
Went to Heaven, of course,
and St. Peter shuffled up to open the gate;
        —Is this Virginia, boy?
            No, ma'am. This here's Heaven.
        Well, it'll have to do.
                    —David Black

Epitaph on a Waiter

    By and by
    God caught his eye.
        —David McCord

Here Lies Sir Tact

Here lies Sir Tact, a diplomatic fellow
Whose silence was not golden, but just yellow.
         —Timothy Steele

An Epitaph

A lovely young lady I mourn in my rhymes:
She was pleasant, good-natured and civil
    sometimes.
Her figure was good; she had very fine eyes;
And her talk was a mixture of foolish and wise.
Her adorers were many, and none of them said,
  She waltzed rather well! It's a pity she's dead!"
         —G. J. Cayley

She Drank Good Ale, Strong Punch and Wine

Epitaph to MRS. FRELAND, *in Edwelton church-yard, Nottinghamshire, 1741*

She drank good ale, strong punch and wine,
And lived to the age of ninety-nine.

—*Anonymous*

Epitaph

Bridget O'Mallow
Here lies asleep.
Her wit was shallow
But her pies were deep.

—*Robert M. Sebastian*

A Smattering of *EARLY LIMERICKS* by the Master Who Created the Form

There Was a Young Person Whose History

There was a young person whose history
Was always considered a mystery;
　　She sate in a ditch,
　　Although no one knew which,
And composed a small treatise on history.

There Was an Old Lady of Chertsey

There was an Old Lady of Chertsey,
Who made a remarkable curtsey;
　　She twirled round and round,

Till she sunk underground,
Which distressed all the people of Chertsey.

There Was an Old Man of Toulouse

There was an old man of Toulouse
Who purchased a new pair of shoes;
    When they asked, "Are they pleasant?"
    He said, "Not at present!"
That turbid old man of Toulouse.

There was a Young Lady of Portugal

There was a Young Lady of Portugal,
Whose ideas were excessively nautical:
    She climbed up a tree,
    To examine the sea,
But declared she would never leave Portugal.

There Was an Old Lady of Winchelsea

There was an old Lady of Winchelsea,
Who said, "If you needle or pin shall see,
  On the floor of my room,
   Sweep it up with the broom!"
That exhaustive old Lady of Winchelsea!

There Was a Young Lady Whose Nose

There was a Young Lady whose nose,
Was so long that it reached to her toes;
  So she hired an Old Lady,
   Whose conduct was steady,
To carry that wonderful nose.

There Was an Old Man in a Boat

There was an Old Man in a boat,
Who said, "I'm afloat! I'm afloat!"
    When they said, "No! you ain't!"
    He was ready to faint,
That unhappy Old Man in a boat.

There Was an Old Man of West Dumpet

There was an old man of West Dumpet,
Who possessed a large nose like a trumpet;
    When he blew it aloud,
    It astonished the crowd,
And was heard through the whole of West
    Dumpet.

—*Edward Lear*

Some Portraits in Miniature, or *SUNDRY LIMERICKS* (This Time Clean Ones)

There Was a Young Lady Called Bright

There was a young lady called Bright
Who would travel faster than light.
    She started one day
    In the relative way
And returned on the previous night.

There Was a Young Maid Who Said, "Why"

There was a young maid who said, "Why
Can't I look in my ear with my eye?
    If I put my mind to it,

I'm sure I can do it.
You never can tell till you try."

There Was an Archdeacon Who Said

There was an Archdeacon who said:
"May I take off my gaiters in bed?"
But the Bishop said: "No,
Wherever you go
You must wear them until you are dead."

There Was a Young Poet of Thusis

There was a young poet of Thusis
Who took twilight walks with the Muses.
But these nymphs of the air
Are not quite what they were,
And the practice has led to abuses.

There Was an Old Man of Boulogne

There was an old man of Boulogne
Who sang a most topical song.
    It wasn't the words
      Which frightened the birds,
But the horrible double-entendre.

There Was an Old Man of Khartoum

There was an old man of Khartoum
Who kept two black sheep in his room.
    "They remind me," he said,
      "Of two friends who are dead,"
But he never would tell us of whom.

There Was an Old Party of Lyme

There was an old party of Lyme
Who married three wives at one time.
 Whey asked: "Why the third?"
 He replied: "One's absurd,
And bigamy, sir, is a crime."

There Was a Young Lady of Lynn

There was a young lady of Lynn
Who was so uncommonly thin
 That when she essayed
 To drink lemonade
She slipped through the straw and fell in.

There Was a Young Man
of Bengal

There was a young man of Bengal
Who went to a fancy-dress ball.
 He went just for fun

Dressed up as a bun,
And a dog ate him up in the hall.

—*Anonymous*

La-Z-Boy—Edmund Clerihew Bentley

Edmund Clerihew Bentley
Was indolent, evidently.
He wasted a great deal of time
Writing this kind of rhyme.

—*Bob McKenty*

FOUR CLERIHEWS
by the Master Who
Invented the Form

George III

George the Third
Ought never to have occurred.
One can only wonder
At so grotesque a blunder.

Savonarola

Savonarola
Declined to wear a bowler,
Expressing the view that it was gammon
To talk of serving God and Mammon.

J. S. Mill

John Stuart Mill,
By a mighty effort of will,
Overcame his natural bonhomie
And wrote "Principles of Political Economy."

Lord Clive

What I like about Clive
Is that he is no longer alive.
There is a great deal to be said
For being dead.

—*Edmund Clerihew Bentley*

from *ACADEMIC GRAFFITI*

Martin Buber

Martin Buber
Never said "Thou" to a tuber:
Despite his creed,
He did not feel the need.

Mary, Queen of Scots

Mary, Queen of Scots,
Could tie the most complicated knots,
But she couldn't bake
The simplest cake.

Henry James

Henry James
Abhorred the word *Dames*,
And always wrote *'Mommas'*
With inverted commas.

—*W. H. Auden*

Quick Flicks *or* Very Short Glances at the Great, the Near Great, & the Sometimes Completely Obscure in *CLERIHEW FORM*

Benjamin Lee Whorf

Benjamin Lee Whorf,
Standing on a London wharf,
Lectured on Language, Thought, & Reality,
Confusing completely the British Admiralty.

Elinor Wylie

Elinor Wylie
Wrote: "My life goes in single filie."
However, after thinking about it for awhile,
Changed it to "My life goes in single file."

George Sand

George Sand
Was no Sally Rand.
George labored at prose.
Sally danced without clothes.

Gertrude Stein

Fine, fine, fine,
Fine, fine,
Fine, fine, fine
Wrote Gertie Stein.

George C. Scott

George C. Scott
Emphatically did not
Sing *William Tell*.
It is probably just as well.

Vivien Leigh

Asked Vivien Leigh
Of Janet Leigh,
"Do you pronounce it 'Lee?
Or Lay?'" Sd. Janet: "Fiddle-dee-dee."

—*Louis Phillips*

FIVE PORTRAITS

Edmund Halley

Edmund Halley
Watched for comets daily.
His success was slight
Till he began watching at night.

Jezebel

The voice of Jezebel
Was more than a decibel
Louder than the dogs who later
Ate her.

P. G. Wodehouse

My clerihew on P. G. Wodehouse
Was based on a rhyme with "Road House."

Oh, no! Too late I learn that it's "Good House"
That rhymes with P. G. Wodehouse.

Christopher Columbus

Christopher Columbus
Discovered tequila, sombreros, tacos, and rumbas.
He said, "We must be in the Orient!"
(Or so the story went.)

Albert Einstein

Albert Einstein
Would occasionally dine
At a night club where
He found thE M.C. square.

—*John Peterson*

TEN

Of Matters Slightly Philosophical

A Man Said to the Universe

A man said to the universe:
"Sir, I exist!"
"However," replied the universe,
"The fact has not created in me
A sense of obligation."

—*Stephen Crane*

The Infinite Regress of Separate Ways

I no longer find it necessary
to tell you

I no longer find it necessary
to tell you

I

—*Morty Schiff*

On the Reason for a Thousand Disputes Ontological, Epistemological, and Other

Belief lies in the tissue,
Not the issue.

—*Morty Schiff*

Philosopher

He scowled at the barometer: "Will it rain?"
None heard, with all that pattering on the pane.

—*John Frederick Nims*

Life

"Life's not worth living, and that's the truth,"
Carelessly caroled the golden youth.
In manhood still he maintained that view
And held it more strongly the older he grew.

When kicked by a jackass at eighty-three,
"Go fetch me a surgeon at once!" cried he.
—*Ambrose Bierce*

O Dear! How Disgusting Is Life!

O dear! How disgusting is life!
To improve it O what can we do?
Most disgusting is hustle and strife,
and of all things an ill-fitting shoe—shoe,
O bother an ill-fitting shoe!
—*Edward Lear*

Human Life

What trifling coil do we poor mortals keep;
Wake, eat, and drink, evacuate, and sleep.
—*Matthew Prior*

Comment

Oh, life is a glorious cycle of song,
A medley of extemporanea;
And love is a thing that can never go wrong;
And I am Marie of Roumania.

—Dorothy Parker

When the Water Went Down

When the water went down, old Noah
Was left with a world to tend—
The same wild seed to nurture,
The same plowshares to mend,
The same chores every morning,
The same wife in his bed,
The same unanswered longing,
The same desire and dread,
But no one to shake his fist at,
No secret cause to gloat.
And Noah yearned for a reason
To build him another boat.

—Barbara K. Loots

I Never Had a Piece of Toast

I never had a piece of toast
Particularly long and wide,
But fell upon the sanded floor,
And always on the buttered side.
            —*James Payn*

The Rain it Raineth

The rain it raineth on the just
    And also on the unjust fella;
But chiefly on the just, because
    The unjust steals the just's umbrella.
            —*Lord Bowen*

On Being Much Better
Than Most and Yet
Not Quite Good Enough

There was a great swimmer named Jack
Who swam ten miles out—and nine back.

—*John Ciardi*

I Wish I Loved the Human Race

I wish I loved the Human Race;
I wish I loved its silly face;
I wish I liked the way it walks;
I wish I liked the way it talks;
And when I'm introduced to one
I wish I thought, "What jolly fun!"

—*Walter A. Raleigh*

Motto

I play it cool
and dig all jive
That's the reason
I stay alive.
My motto,
As I live and learn,
            is:
Dig and Be Dug
In Return.

—*Langston Hughes*

The Optimist

When the world is all against you;
When the race of life is run;
When the skies have turned to gray again—
Just say, "I've had me fun."
When the friends of yore all turn away
And sadness is the rule,
Just say, "The skies will turn again"—
You silly, bloody fool!

—*Anonymous*
(English Music Hall Song)

310

On the World

The world's an inn; and I her guest.
I eat; I drink; I take my rest.
My hostess, Nature, does deny me
Nothing, wherewith she can supply me;
Where, having stayed a while, I pay
Her lavish bills, and go my way.
—*Francis Quarles*

Borrowing

(from the French)

Some of the hurts you have cured,
And the sharpest you still have survived,
But what torments of grief you endured
From evils which never arrived!
—*Ralph Waldo Emerson*

Where Is the Je-M'en-Fichisme of Yesterday?

Some thirty years ago
  (More, if you quibble)
The universal *mot*
  Was "ish kabibble."

We let the world go by;
  Its foolish flurry
Evoked the cheery cry
  Of "I should worry."

In that exultant day
  We saw no good of
Worrying life away.
  Perhaps we should've.
        —*Morris Bishop*

For Those Who
Always Fear the Worst

Suppose one thing,
Suppose another,
Suppose your mother
Was a bullfrog's brother.
      —*Anonymous*

Theology

God is the unmoved Mover. Thus we prove
His changeless nature: never to improve.
      —*X. J. Kennedy*

Zander on God

It may not cover all theodicy
Or make him popular among the seraphim,
But "If God were true," my Zander said to me,
"He wouldn't make people not believe in Him."
      —*Howard Nemerov*

313

The Book of Wisdom

Thou shalt not commit adultery;
Nor shalt thou covet thy neighbor's spouse.
Shouldst thou succumb to temptation, thou
Shalt not covet in thy neighbor's house.
                    —*Kenneth Leonhardt*

Eight Cents Cotton

Eight cents cotton an' thutty cents meat,
How in de worl' kin a po' man eat?
                    —*Anonymous*
          (American Folk Rhyme)

Money

Money is a kind of poetry.
                    —*Wallace Stevens*

Money, the long green,
cash, stash, rhino, jack
or just plain dough.

Chock it up, fork it over,
shell it out. Watch it
burn holes through pockets.

To be made of it! To have it
to burn! Greenbacks, double eagles,
megabucks and Ginnie Maes.

It greases the palm, feathers a nest,
holds heads above water,
makes both ends meet.

Money breeds money.
Gathering interest, compounding daily.
Always in circulation.

Money. You don't know where it's been,
but you put it where your mouth is.
And it talks.

—*Dana Gioia*

Wilt Thou Lend Me Thy Mare?

Wilt thou lend me thy mare to go a mile?
No, she's lamed leaping over a stile.

But if thou wilt her to me spare
Thou shalt have money for thy mare.

O, O, say you so?
Money will make the mare to go.
Money will make the mare to go.

—*Anonymous*

De White Folks Git de Money

De ole bee make de honey-comb,
De young bee make de honey,
De black mens make de cotton en co'n,
En de w'ite folks git de money.

—*Joel Chandler Harris*

from *The Wants of Man*

"Man wants but little here below,
  Nor wants that little long."
'Tis not with me exactly so.
  But 'tis so in the song.
My wants are many, and if told
  Would muster many a score,
And were each with a mint of gold,
  I still should long for more.

  —*John Quincy Adams*

I Was a Stranger

"I was a stranger, and you took me in."
  So spake the Christ; and you seemed kind as He.
  When I was hungered, short of do-re-mi,
You offered introductions—credit—gin—
The shirt from off your back, come lose, come win;
  Your eyes were wet from selfless sympathy.
"I was a stranger, and you took me in."
  So spake the Christ; and you seemed kind as He.

I woke next morning, gulped down aspirin,
    And found you gone, and gone your charity . . .
    Also my wallet, credit cards, and key.
It's odd, in fact, that I still have my skin.
I was a stranger, and you took me in.

—*Willard Espy*

Infant Innocence

The Grizzly Bear is huge and wild;
He has devoured the infant child.
The infant child is not aware
He has been eaten by the bear.

—*A.E.Housman*

Thoughts While Serving on a Jury

When I was young in that green time
Between B.C. and now,
And rhymed to live and lived to rhyme
And loved the girls like chow,
And thoughts of what I *couldn't* get,

Disturbed not what I got,
And life was like the alphabet,
Why, I was young—so what?
                    —*Samuel Hoffenstein*

from *A Short Song of Congratulation*

Long-expected one and twenty
    Lingering year at last is flown,
Pomp and pleasure, pride and plenty
    Great Sir John, are all your own.

Loosened from the minor's tether,
    Free to mortgage or to sell,
Wild as wind, and light as feather,
    Bid the slaves of thrift farewell.

Call the Bettys, Kates, and Jennys,
    Every name that laughs at care,
Lavish of your grandsire's guineas,
    Show the spirit of an heir.
                    —*Samuel Johnson*

Caution to Old Age

An empty brain, an active tongue,
Are more attractive in the young.
—*Laurence Perrine*

Experience

To one who, journeying through night and fog,
Is mired neck-deep in an unwholesome bog,
Experience, like the rising of the dawn,
Reveals the path that he should not have gone.
—*Ambrose Bierce*

On Coming to Nothing

Old friends, nearing senility,
we sit, every last prospect dim,
and think: The world was wrong about me . .
but at least it was right about him.

—Richard Moore

Lines by an Old Fogy

I'm thankful that the sun and moon
   Are both hung up so high,
That no presumptuous hand can stretch
   And pull them from the sky.

If they were not, I have no doubt
   But some reforming ass
Would recommend to take them down
   And light the world with gas.

—Anonymous

My Granddad

My granddad, viewing earth's worn cogs,
Said things were going to the dogs;
His granddad in his house of logs,
Said things were going to the dogs;
His granddad in the Flemish bogs
Said things were going to the dogs;
His granddad in his old skin togs,
Said things were going to the dogs;

There's one thing that I have to state—
The dogs have had a good long wait.

—Anonymous

A Reflection on
the Course of Human Life

My younger years I did employ
in trifling pleasure's empty joy:
my riper days consumèd were
in anxious frets and carking care:
and in old age I scarce could borrow

a moment's rest from pain and sorrow.
This medley race of joy, care, sorrow, pain,
Lord! who would wish to run it o'er again.
                    —William Lloyd

On the Vanity of
Earthly Greatness

The tusks that clashed in mighty brawls
Of mastodons, are billiard balls.

The sword of Charlemagne the Just
Is ferric oxide, known as rust.

The grizzly bear whose potent hug
Was feared by all, is now a rug.

Great Caesar's bust is on the shelf,
And I don't feel so well myself.
                    —Arthur Guiterman

Aftermath

Funeral expenses
will have you, in wonder, taking
leave of your senses
at such an undertaking.
—*Edmund Conti*

Résumé

Razors pain you;
Rivers are damp;
Acids stain you;
And drugs cause cramp.
Guns aren't lawful;
Nooses give;
Gas smells awful;
You might as well live.
—*Dorothy Parker*

Waste

I had written to Aunt Maud,
Who was on a trip abroad,
When I heard she'd died of cramp
Just too late to save the stamp.

—*Harry Graham*

Hope

He rose up on his dying bed
and asked for fish.
His wife looked it up in her dream book
and played it.

—*Langston Hughes*

My Own Epitaph

Life is a jest, and all things show it;
I thought so once, but now I know it.

—*John Gay*

Well-Preserved

A lady, out of sorts with Fate,
Grew weary and disconsolate,
And periodically tried
To find relief in suicide
From problems that involved her heart.
But every time she made a start
With gas or razor blades or dope
Or odd, assorted lengths of rope,
The telephone would ring, and then
She'd answer, full of hope again,
That her uncertain darling might
Perhaps be coming round that night.
And so between despair and rage
She lingered to a ripe old age.

—Margaret Fishback

Black Track

There are so many other ways
    Of making graceful bows.
What's wrong with gas or gun or rope
    Or trampling by wild cows?

326

Please note for future use, there's
  Poison, river, sword or dirk.
Don't jump in front of subway trains
  And make me late for work.

—*Alma Denny*

The Flaw in Paganism

Drink and dance and laugh and lie,
  Love, the reeling midnight through,
For tomorrow we shall die!
  (But, alas, we never do.)

—*Dorothy Parker*

from *My Last Will*

When I am safely laid away,
Out of work and out of play,
Sheltered by the kindly ground
From the world of sight and sound,
One or two of those I leave
Will remember me and grieve,
Thinking how I made them gay

By the things I used to say;
—But the crown of their distress
Will be my untidiness.

What a nuisance then will be
All that shall remain of me!
Shelves of books I never read,
Piles of bills, undocketed,
Shaving-brushes, razors, strops,
Bottles that have lost their tops,
Boxes full of odds and ends,
Letters from departed friends,
Faded ties and broken braces
Tucked away in secret places,
Baggy trousers, ragged coats,
Stacks of ancient lecture-notes,
And that ghostliest of shows,
Boots and shoes in horrid rows.
Though they are of cheerful mind,
My lovers, whom I leave behind,
When they find these in my stead,
Will be sorry I am dead.
        —*Walter A. Raleigh*

Reflections of a Curmudgeon

On Doctors:
Their training's tough, but by and large
What some learn best is how to charge.

On Dentists:
The pain they cause will seem banal
Until you need a root canal.

On Lawyers:
Think twice before you trust your fate
To those who urge: "Let's litigate."

On Brokers:
At certain times their streaks are hot
But seldom when the market's not.

On Baseball Players:
Paid more than a Wall St. broker,
Most prove less than mediocre.

On Politicians:
Those whose tongues are sugar-coated
Love to claim they've been misquoted.

On Actors:
The temperamental ones offstage
Are those who cannot act their age.

On Editors:
Though some are viewed as prince or priest,
I like those best who edit least.

On Poets:
Most heavyweights are one dull breed,
But light verse wits are fun to read.

—*Ned Pastor*

from *Essay on Criticism*

True wit is Nature to advantage dressed,
What oft was thought, but ne'er so well expressed;
Something worse truth convinced at sight we find,
That gives us back the image of our mind.
As shades more sweetly recommend the light,
So modest plainness sets off sprightly wit;
For works may have more wit than does them good,
As bodies perish through excess of blood.

—*Alexander Pope*

Cajolery

Cajolery works, but you've got to know how.
Pulling its leg won't get milk from a cow.
—*John Frederick Nims*

Virtue and Vice

Virtue and Vice look much the same,
If Truth is naked, so is Shame.
—*W. S. Landor*

Couplet for a Dog's Collar

I am his Highness' Dog at Kew;
Pray tell me, Sir, whose Dog are you?
—*Alexander Pope*

Delight in Disorder

A sweet disorder in the dress
Kindles in clothes a wantonness.
A lawn about the shoulders thrown
Into a fine distraction;
An erring lace, which here and there
Enthralls the crimson stomacher;
A cuff neglectful, and thereby
Ribbons to flow confusedly;
A winning wave, deserving note,
In the tempestuous petticoat;
A careless shoestring, in whose tie
I see a wild civility;
Do more bewitch me than when art
Is too precise in every part.

—*Robert Herrick*

Lover Boy

Narcissus was too perfect for sex or pelf—
He longed only to gaze in love at himself . . .
The moral of which is that, even in myths,
Too much reflection may be your nemesis.

—*Kenneth Leonhardt*

Index of Authors

333

335

Copyrights and Permissions

337

338